701 Lebanese Verbs

701 Lebanese Verbs

By

Maroun G. Kassab

First Published in the United States of America on January 1, 2013
By Black Pinnacle LLC

ISBN-13: 978-0615751245 (Black Pinnacle LLC)

Cover, back cover and page design by Maroun Kassab

Contents

Introduction

The verbs in the Lebanese language could be classified into Verb Groups. These groups govern how almost every verb in the Lebanese language behaves. This makes the amount of irregular verbs very small, not to say negligible. The Lebanese language is very specific in terms of how verbs sound and how they rhyme in their sounds. This "rhyme" governs which group a verb belongs to. Therefore, when a verb rhymes with a certain verb group, it will conjugate through all its tenses according to the rules of that group.

This group classification makes several determinations on how the Lebanese verbs should be organized. With a total lack of any previous research or classification system to fall back upon, this book is somewhat a groundbreaking research. This does not mean that I am setting things in stone when it comes to the classification of the Lebanese verbs. It is simply a personal approach to verb classification based on several years of research into the inner workings of the Lebanese language. There might be a different approach, and maybe even a better approach. Yet at this point, and with the information at hand, this is in my opinion the best way to go about classifying the Lebanese verbs.

In addition, a classification system is not possible without a standardized system of writing. Therefore, this book uses the Lebanese Latin Letters system (LLL) devised by the Lebanese Language Institute as a writing model for the Lebanese language. In addition, a standardized spelling system utilizing the alphabet is adopted to write all Lebanese words in this book. You will find a table that shows the Lebanese alphabet according to this system at the end of this introduction. For an audio of all these sounds you can visit the website of the author of this book at **www.studylebanese.com** to hear how each letter is spelled.

Before we venture to understand how verbs are conjugated in the Lebanese language a couple or remarks must be made about what this book is about, and more importantly, about what this book is not about. This book elucidates the various verb groups in the Lebanese language with examples on the conjugation of a representative verb from each group through all the provided tenses. This book is not about teaching the difference between verb states and their inner relationships. Having said this, I feel that it is still necessary to give a quick look into one important aspect of Lebanese verbs.

In the Lebanese language, there are three types of relationships for verbs:

1- A passive relationship
2- A projective relationship
3- An injective relationship

Let us consider the following diagram:

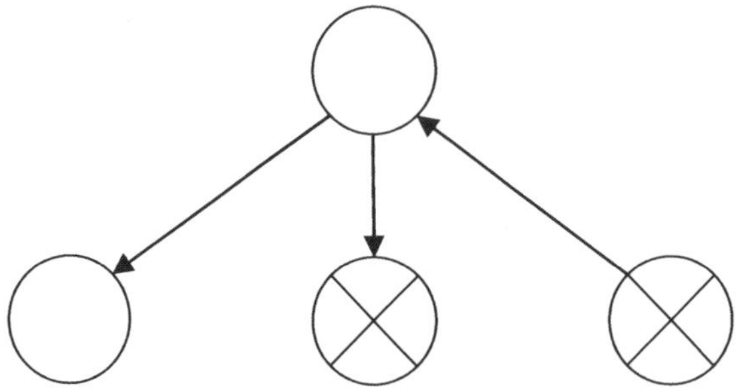

Diagram 1

If the circle is the subject of the sentence, and the circle with an X is someone or something else, the action the verb designates is either:

1- Passive: Example: I woke up (wxiit)
2- Projective: Example: I woke Mark up (waxxayt)
3- Injective: I was woken up by Sandra (twaxxayt)

In the first case, the action is exerted by the subject on itself. In the second case, the action is exerted by the subject on someone or something else and in the third example the action is exerted on the subject by someone on something else. These three fundamental actions are important to understand how the verbs behave in the Lebanese language. Whereas in English the verb "wake" is the same, in Lebanese, these are three different verb forms and each of them conjugates with the personal pronouns under a different verb category. Moreover, not every verb has all three verb states, but it will always have two, usually an injective case, and either a passive or a projective case.

But, though you need to understand this difference, you will not need to worry much about telling the differences between these verbs, because each type will be treated as a completely separate verb. In the verb classification, you should pay attention to how the verb is translated, and this will give you a clue whether this verb is passive, projective or injective verb.

Teaching Methods

There are various methods to teach the verbs in the Lebanese language. There is also a traditional way to teach verbs in almost all Semitic languages. Verbs in Semitic languages can be traced to what is usually referred to as a "verb root". Verb roots are usually 3 or 4 letter consonants.

For example:

Harab: HRB (Escaped)
Ḱarbac: ḰRBC (Scribbled)

This method, although useful to know, was devised because of a very important reason. The structure of Semitic alphabets does not have "vowels". Therefore, these languages are written using a consonant system only. There are three sounds that are referred to as "aȟrof xilli" in Arabic for example, that have a proximity to what a vowel is, but do not perform the same function. But, since we are writing the Lebanese language using a Latin alphabet, a different method utilizing the existence of a varied vowels system in the new Latin alphabet has been followed to classify the verbs.

The Lebanese language in general and the verbs in particular are very musical. This makes them easy to learn. Therefore, the verb tables in this book will include rhyming verb categories that will commit to your memory the musicality of the conjugation of the representative verbs in each tense. These tables, if memorized and used, will save much trouble, and will assist in pronouncing and using the verbs in the Lebanese language properly.

The 68 verb categories that are conjugated in the tables in this book are representative of almost all the verbs in the Lebanese language. At the end of the book, you will find a list of most common verbs that will refer in their conjugation to one of these verb groups. On the back of this page you will find an alphabet table that explains the letters and their pronunciation in this book.

Remark: As with any verbs conjugation book, this book is intended to provide verb conjugation with the Subject Personal Pronouns only. To extend the conjugation beyond that point would exceed the scope of this book.

The Lebanese Alphabet

The Letter		Solar/ Lunar	Pronunciation in English	2 Examples in Lebanese	Their Meaning in English
` (Alef)	`a	Lunar	The beginning sound in "If"	`mar, War`a	Moons, Paper
A	A	Lunar	A in Car or Cat	Alam, Mara	Pencil, Woman
B	Be	Lunar	B in Bed	Balad, Trab	Country, Soil
C	Ce	Solar	Sh in She	Cajra, Micwar	Tree, Trip
D	De	Solar	D in Door	Dibb, Adab	Bear, Literature
Ḋ	Ḋa	Solar	Hard D	Ḋaw, Bayḋa	Light, Egg
E	Ee	Lunar	"a" in care or "ai" in fair	Elib, Wled	Cast, Children
F	Fe	Lunar	F in frog	Faara, Caraf	Mouse, Honor
G	Ge	Lunar	G in Glass	Gilal, Argiili	Marbles, Water pipe
Ġ	Ġe	Lunar	G without closing air flow	Ġariib, Ciġil	Strange, Work
H	Ha	Lunar	H in home	Hawa, Nahir	Air, River
Ḣ	Ḣa	Lunar	Hard H	Ḣilo, Baḣir	Beautiful, Sea
I	I	Lunar	I in Intersect	Imm, Sini	Mother, Year
II	II	Lunar	"ee" in feed or "ea" in seal	Iid, Akiid	Hand, Sure
J	Je	Solar	G in Beige (without d sound)	Jabal, Rijjel	Mountain, Man
K	Ke	Lunar	K in book	Kalib, Akil	Dog, Food
Ḱ	Ḱa	Lunar	J in Spanish, Ch in German	Ḱibiz, Taḱit	Bread, Bed
L	Le	Solar	L in land	Laban, Walad	Yogurt, Child
M	Me	Lunar	M in man	Mreyi, Namli	Mirror, Ant
N	Ne	Solar	N in name	Naḣli, Janni	Bee, Paradise
O	O	Lunar	O in open	Oroppa, Loz	Europe, Almond
P	Pe	Lunar	P in Peter	Pliiz, Flipper	Please, Pinball
Q	Qa	Lunar	Hard K	Qaarra, Iqaax	Continent, Rhythm
R	Ra	Solar	R in orange	Raas, Mrabba	Head, Jam
S	Sa	Solar	S in Sam	Samki, Rasmi	Fish, Drawing
Ṡ	Ṡa	Solar	Hard S	Ṡura, Raṡiif	Picture, Pavement
T	Te	Solar	T in toy	Talij, Zaytun	Snow, Olive
Ṫ	Ṫa	Solar	Hard T	Ṫawiil, Maṫaar	Tall, Airport
U	U	Lunar	oo in moon, u in June	Uḋa, Ṫawus	Room, Peacock
V	Ve	Lunar	V in Victor	Viidyo, Bravo	Video, Bravo
W	We	Lunar	W in word	Wardi, Maw`af	Flower, Parking
X	Xa	Lunar	A stretching tongue base	Xacra, Lixbi	Ten, Toy
Y	Ye	Lunar	Y in yellow	Yamiin, Laymun	Right, Oranges
Z	Ze	Solar	Z in Zebra	Zġiir, Lawzi	Small, Almond
Ż	Ża	Solar	Hard Z	Żarif, Buża	Envelope, Ice cream

The Essentials

A- The Personal Pronouns:

There are eight Subject Personal Pronouns (SPP) in the Lebanese language and this is what we will be conjugating all the verbs with. The SPP in the Lebanese language have a dual meaning. The pronoun "Huwwi" for instance could mean "He" or "He is". For example:

"Huwwi" akal means "He ate"

"Huwwi Mark" means "He is Mark"

As you can see, this dual meaning actually simplifies the language process.

Below is a table of the Subject Personal Pronouns:

Pronoun	Meaning 1	Meaning 2	Number and Gender
Ana	I	I am	Singular Masculine
Inta	You	You are	Singular Masculine
Inti	You	You are	Singular Feminine
Into	You	You are	Plural
Huwwi	He	He is	Singular Masculine
Hiyyi	She	She is	Singular Feminine
Hinni	They	They are	Plural
Niħna	We	We are	Plural

The SPP are not used very often, because the verbs themselves usually carry the meaning of the suggested pronoun they represent.

B- Supplements:

Conjugation supplements are terms that are used to create tenses. Supplements also are terms that are not necessarily verbs in the true sense of the word, but are rather "supplementary verbs" that give meaning to sentences.

1- Xam

This term is a supplement to the continuous tense. For example, the Present Continuous tense is composed of the term "xam" plus the infinitive. "Xam" is also used with the past continuous tense as well. In short, it is a term that indicates the continuous state.

For example:

Niħna xam nitġadda: We are dining

2- Raħ

"Raħ" means "will" or "shall". In addition, when it is combined with the past tense of verb "to be", it could mean "would". It is used to indicate the future tense.

For example:

Ana raħ nem: I will sleep
Inti kinti raħ tcufi Mark: You would have seen Mark

3- Lezim

"Lezim" means "must". When it is combined with the past tense of verb "to be", it could mean "should". It is used to indicate the future tense.

For example:

Inta lezim tekol: You must eat
Inti ken lezim truħi mberiħ: You should have left yesterday

We will only be using "raħ" in this book, and then you can easily exchange "raħ" for "lezim" if needed.

Verb Forms

The verb tenses conjugated in this book are not all that are present in the Lebanese language. There are some more complicated tenses, but they are derivatives of the tenses that are conjugated in this book. The tenses that are not discussed in this book are rarely used, and a student of the Lebanese language would hardly encounter any of these forms in everyday conversation. The forms that are conjugated here are the following:

a- The Infinitive
b- Simple Present
c- Perfect Present
d- Simple Past
e- Imperative
f- Past Continuous
g- Past Habit
h- Past Perfect
i- Past Anterior
j- Present Continuous
k- Simple Future
l- Anterior Future

Of the above tenses, the first five are the principal forms and the remaining are composed structures of these five forms.

A- The Infinitive:

The infinitive verb form is an essential ingredient in many conjugated verb forms. Yet, the infinitive verb form rarely occurs by itself. It is neither used in direct connection with the pronoun. For example you cannot say "Ana idhan"; such a statement would not have any meaning. The infinitive form only becomes meaningful when it is a conjugation element with other verb tenses. This form is part of the following main verb forms:

a- Past Continuous
b- Past Habit
c- Present Continuous
d- Simple Future
e- Anterior Future

B- The Simple Present:

The Simple Present tense is used to describe actions that are factual or habitual.

For example:

Btitloj bil Arz kill sini: It snows in the Cedars every year.
L xaṡfur biṫiir: The bird flies

C- The Perfect Present:

The Perfect Present tense has a triple function. First, it means that something has been done or perfected in the past.

For example:

Huwwi mitzallij min abil: He has skied before

The second function is not comprehensive to all Present Perfect tense forms. This function indicates an action that has started somewhere in the past and is extending into the present. In this sense, it is confused with the Present Continuous. This is not to say that this confusion is without merit, because this tense is used to express the Present Continuous condition. The difference between this tense and the present continuous tense will be elucidated in that section, which is Section J.

For example:

Ana felil: I am leaving

The third function is that this tense can also suggest the future:

For example:

Ana raayiḣ baxd noṡṡ sexa: I am leaving in half an hour

D- The Simple Past:

The Simple Past indicates an action in the past relative to the speaker.

For example:

Hiyyi aḱadit l mifteḣ: She took the key

E- The Imperative:

The Imperative is a command that is given to someone. In this sense, it is only used with the pronoun "You", whether masculine or feminine, singular or plural.

For example:

Umi: Get up
Jiib: Bring

F- The Past Continuous:

The Past Continuous indicates a continuous action that was happening at some point in the past.

For example:

Inta kint xam tekol: You were eating
Inti kinti xam tilxabi: You were playing

G- The Past Habit:

The Past Habit indicates a habitual action that used to happen in the past.

For example:

Hinni keno yeklo bass ḱoḋra: They used to eat only vegetables

H- The Past Perfect:

The Past Perfect indicates that an action was in the process of happening in the past before something else happened.

For example:

Niḣna kinna felliin lamma woṡil Mark: We were leaving when Mark arrived

I- The Past Anterior:

The Past Anterior indicates either a conditional action that relied on the happening of a past condition, or an action that was completed in the past before something else happened in the past.

For example:

Huwwi <u>ken ija</u> law ken maxo siyyaara: He would have come if he had a car
Hiyyi <u>kenit nemit</u> abil ma tġiib ccams: She had slept before sunset

J- Present Continuous:

The Present Continuous indicates continuing action, something in the process of happening.

For example:

Inti <u>xam t`uli</u> inno Mark ken hawn: You are saying that Mark was here.

To understand better the difference between the present continuous tense and the present perfect tense in Lebanese we shall look at the following two examples:

1- Ana <u>xam u`af</u> (I am standing): Present Continuous
2- Ana <u>we`if</u> (I am standing): Present Perfect

In the first example, the sense of the statement "I am standing" indicates that the process of "getting up" is in progress. The second statement indicates that the process of getting up is finished, and that I already stood up, and I am "still standing".

K- Simple Future:

The Simple Future tense indicates that an action is in the future relative to the speaker.

For example:

Into <u>raḣ tnemo</u> xind Mark: You will sleep at Mark's place

L- Anterior Future:

The Anterior Future indicates a conditional action that could have happened in the past.

For example:

Huwwi <u>ken raḣ yu`ax</u> law ma miskito Sandra: He would have fallen if Sandra would not have caught him.

Essential Auxiliary Verbs

In the Lebanese language, there are auxiliary verbs that are used in conjunction with other verbs to generate meaning and to create conjugations. The four main auxiliary verbs that will be presented in this book are:

1- To be : Ykun
2- Can: Fii
3- To Want: Baddo
4- To Have: Maxo and Xindo

These four verbs are essential in every language.

1- Verb "Ykun"

Verb "To be" is used to create several conjugations in the Lebanese language. This verb is used to create the following verb tenses:

a- Past Continuous
b- Past Habit
c- Past Perfect
d- Past Anterior
e- Anterior Future

In addition, forms of this verb are used to create more complex verb tenses.

For example:

Ana kint raȟ kun xam bilxab: I would have been playing.

But, as we discussed earlier, these more complex conjugations are not part of this book. Maybe in the future, a more expanded version of verb conjugations will be available, but for the requirements of this book, the provided conjugations are more than sufficient.

On the following page, you will find the conjugation for the verb "to be" in all the tenses presented in this book.

Ykun

To be

Group: 4Eb

Principal Forms

Pronoun	Infinitive	Simple Present	Perfect Present	Simple Past	Imperative
Ana	kun	bkun	keyin	kint	
Inta	tkun	bitkun	keyin	kint	kun
Inti	tkuni	bitkuni	keyni	kinti	kuni
Into	tkuno	bitkuno	keyniin	kinto	kuno
Huwwi	ykun	bikun	keyin	ken	
Hiyyi	tkun	bitkun	keyni	kenit	
Hinni	ykuno	bikuno	keyniin	keno	
Niħna	nkun	minkun	keyniin	kinna	

Past Tense Forms

Pronoun + To Be		Past Continuous		Past Habit	Past Perfect	Past Anterior
Ana	kint	xam	kun	kun	keyin	kint
Inta	kint	xam	tkun	tkun	keyin	kint
Inti	kinti	xam	tkuni	tkuni	keyni	kinti
Into	kinto	xam	tkuno	tkuno	keyniin	kinto
Huwwi	ken	xam	ykun	ykun	keyin	ken
Hiyyi	kenit	xam	tkun	tkun	keyni	kenit
Hinni	keno	xam	ykuno	ykuno	keyniin	keno
Niħna	kinna	xam	nkun	nkun	keyniin	kinna

Present and Future Tense Forms

Pronoun	Present Continuous		Simple Future		Anterior Future	
Ana	xam	kun	raħ	kun	kint raħ	kun
Inta	xam	tkun	raħ	tkun	kint raħ	tkun
Inti	xam	tkuni	raħ	tkuni	kinti raħ	tkuni
Into	xam	tkuno	raħ	tkuno	kinto raħ	tkuno
Huwwi	xam	ykun	raħ	ykun	ken raħ	ykun
Hiyyi	xam	tkun	raħ	tkun	kenit raħ	tkun
Hinni	xam	ykuno	raħ	ykuno	keno raħ	ykuno
Niħna	xam	nkun	raħ	nkun	kinna raħ	nkun

Notes
The form "ken" alone of verb "ykun" is used with the other auxiliary verbs to generate the past tense for these verbs.

2- Verb "Fii"

"Fii" means "can". This verb is an auxiliary verb that only has a single verb form and does not conjugate into other verb tenses. When combined with the past tense of verb "to be", it acquires a "past tense" state.

The following table shows how this verb conjugates with the Subject Personal Pronouns:

Pronoun	**Verb**	**Meaning**	**With Verb "to be"**	**Meaning**
Ana	fiyyi	I can	ken fiyyi	I could have
Inta	fiik	You can	ken fiik	You could have
Inti	fiiki	You can	ken fiiki	You could have
Into	fiikon	You can	ken fiikon	You could have
Huwwi	fii	He can	ken fii	He could have
Hiyyi	fiya	She can	ken fiya	She could have
Hinni	fiyon	They can	ken fiyon	They could have
Niħna	fiina	We can	ken fiina	We could have

3- Verb "Baddo"

"Baddo" means "to want". This verb is another auxiliary verb that only has a single verb form and does not conjugate into other verb tenses. Similar to "fii", when combined with the past tense of verb "to be", it acquires a "past tense" state.

The following table shows how this verb conjugates with the Subject Personal Pronouns:

Pronoun	**Verb**	**Meaning**	**With Verb "to be"**	**Meaning**
Ana	baddi	I want	ken baddi	I wanted
Inta	baddak	You want	ken baddak	You wanted
Inti	baddik	You want	ken baddik	You wanted
Into	baddkon	You want	ken baddkon	You wanted
Huwwi	baddo	He wants	ken baddo	He wanted
Hiyyi	badda	She wants	ken badda	She wanted
Hinni	baddon	They want	ken baddon	They wanted
Niħna	baddna	We want	ken baddna	We wanted

4- Verbs "Maxo" and "Xindo"

These two verbs mean "have". They are the third and fourth auxiliary verbs that only have a single verb form and do not conjugate into other verb tenses. Similar to "fii" and "baddo", when combined with the past tense of verb "to be", they acquire a "past tense" state.

The following tables show how these verbs conjugate with the Subject Personal Pronouns:

Pronoun	Verb	Meaning	With Verb "to be"	Meaning
Ana	maxi	I have	ken maxi	I had
Inta	maxak	You have	ken maxak	You had
Inti	maxik	You have	ken maxik	You had
Into	maxkon	You have	ken maxkon	You had
Huwwi	maxo	He has	ken maxo	He had
Hiyyi	maxa	She has	ken maxa	She had
Hinni	maxon	They have	ken maxon	They had
Niħna	maxna	We have	ken maxna	We had

Pronoun	Verb	Meaning	With Verb "to be"	Meaning
Ana	xindi	I have	ken xindi	I had
Inta	xindak	You have	ken xindak	You had
Inti	xindik	You have	ken xindik	You had
Into	xindkon	You have	ken xindkon	You had
Huwwi	xindo	He has	ken xindo	He had
Hiyyi	xinda	She has	ken xinda	She had
Hinni	xindon	They have	ken xindon	They had
Niħna	xinna	We have	ken xinna	We had

The difference between "maxo" and "xindo" is subtle. "Maxo" means that you have something "on hand" "right now", whereas "xindo" expresses "ownership" in general terms. For example, "maxi alam" means that I have a pen on me right now, whereas "xindi alam" means that I have a pen, but it is for example at home, and not necessarily on me right now.

How to use the tables

The verbs in this book are divided into groups. These groups are based on the number of letters that are present in the infinitive form of the verb. So group 4 for example will contain verbs whose infinitive form is composed out of 4 letters. This applies to all verbs in this book. The main group is then divided into subgroups. These subgroups are dependent on the location of the consonants and vowels in the infinitive form of the verbs. This classification simplifies things, because once you have a verb that needs to be conjugated, you can locate the group it falls under and then simply substitute the consonants of the example verb in the group with the consonants of that verb. Let us say that you want to conjugate the verb "**ysexid**" which means "to help". If we look this verb up in the tables, we find that it belongs to group 6F. We then go to group 6F and look at the existing example, "**yjewib**", which means "to answer":

Yjewib:

Pronoun	Infinitive	Simple Present	Perfect Present	Simple Past	Imperative
Ana	jewib	bjewib	mjewib	jewabt	
Inta	tjewib	bitjewib	mjewib	jewabt	jewib
Inti	tjewbi	bitjewbi	mjewbi	jewabti	jewbi
Into	tjewbo	bitjewbo	mjewbiin	jewabto	jewbo
Huwwi	yjewib	bijewib	mjewib	jewab	
Hiyyi	tjewib	bitjewib	mjewbi	jewabit	
Hinni	yjewbo	bijewbo	mjewbiin	jewabo	
Niħna	njewib	minjewib	mjewbiin	jewabna	

If we analyze this verb we will see that it contains two vowels, the "e" and the "i". If we then look at the verb "ysexid", we will realize that it also contains the two vowels "e" and "i". The difference here is the consonants. So, by replacing each consonant by the corresponding consonant:

Y	J	E	W	I	B
Y	S	E	X	I	D

You will end up with this table:

Principle Forms

Pronoun	Infinitive	Simple Present	Perfect Present	Simple Past	Imperative
Ana	sexid	bsexid	msexid	sexadt	
Inta	tsexid	bitsexid	msexid	sexadt	sexid
Inti	tsexdi	bitsexdi	msexdi	sexadti	sexdi
Into	tsexdo	bitsexdo	msexdiin	sexadto	sexdo
Huwwi	ysexid	bisexid	msexid	sexad	
Hiyyi	tsexid	bitsexid	msexdi	sexadit	
Hinni	ysexdo	bisexdo	msexdiin	sexado	
Niħna	nsexid	minsexid	msexdiin	sexadna	

And once you have this table, you have the rest of the conjugations:

Past Tense Forms

Pronoun + To Be		Past Continuous		Past Habit	Past Perfect	Past Anterior
Ana	**kint**	xam	sexid	sexid	msexid	sexadt
Inta	**kint**	xam	tsexid	tsexid	msexid	sexadt
Inti	**kinti**	xam	tsexdi	tsexdi	msexdi	sexadti
Into	**kinto**	xam	tsexdo	tsexdo	msexdiin	sexadto
Huwwi	**ken**	xam	ysexid	ysexid	msexid	sexad
Hiyyi	**kenit**	xam	tsexid	tsexid	msexdi	sexadit
Hinni	**keno**	xam	ysexdo	ysexdo	msexdiin	sexado
Niħna	**kinna**	xam	nsexid	nsexid	msexdiin	sexadna

Present and Future Tense Forms

Pronoun	Present Continuous		Simple Future		Anterior Future	
Ana	xam	sexid	raħ	sexid	kint raħ	sexid
Inta	xam	tsexid	raħ	tsexid	kint raħ	tsexid
Inti	xam	tsexdi	raħ	tsexdi	kinti raħ	tsexdi
Into	xam	tsexdo	raħ	tsexdo	kinto raħ	tsexdo
Huwwi	xam	ysexid	raħ	ysexid	ken raħ	ysexd
Hiyyi	xam	tsexid	raħ	tsexid	kenit raħ	tsexid
Hinni	xam	ysexdo	raħ	ysexdo	keno raħ	ysexdo
Niħna	xam	nsexid	raħ	nsexid	kinna raħ	nsexid

Verb Conjugations and Groups

Yiji

To come

Group: 4A

Principal Forms

Pronoun	Infinitive	Simple Present	Perfect Present	Simple Past	Imperative
Ana	iji	biji	jeyi	jiit	
Inta	tiji	btiji	jeyi	jiit	tax
Inti	tiji	btiji	jeyi	jiiti	taxi
Into	tijo	btijo	jeyiin	jiito	taxo
Huwwi	yiji	byiji	jeyi	ija	
Hiyyi	tiji	btiji	jeyi	ijit	
Hinni	yijo	byijo	jeyiin	ijo	
Niħna	niji	mniji	jeyiin	jiina	

Past Tense Forms

Pronoun + To Be		Past Continuous		Past Habit	Past Perfect	Past Anterior
Ana	kint	xam	iji	iji	jeyi	jiit
Inta	kint	xam	tiji	tiji	jeyi	jiit
Inti	kinti	xam	tiji	tiji	jeyi	jiiti
Into	kinto	xam	tijo	tijo	jeyiin	jiito
Huwwi	ken	xam	yiji	yiji	jeyi	ija
Hiyyi	kenit	xam	tiji	tiji	jeyi	ijit
Hinni	keno	xam	yijo	yijo	jeyiin	ijo
Niħna	kinna	xam	niji	niji	jeyiin	jiina

Present and Future Tense Forms

Pronoun	Present Continuous		Simple Future		Anterior Future	
Ana	xam	iji	raħ	iji	kint raħ	iji
Inta	xam	tiji	raħ	tiji	kint raħ	tiji
Inti	xam	tiji	raħ	tiji	kinti raħ	tiji
Into	xam	tijo	raħ	tijo	kinto raħ	tijo
Huwwi	xam	yiji	raħ	yiji	ken raħ	yiji
Hiyyi	xam	tiji	raħ	tiji	kenit raħ	tiji
Hinni	xam	yijo	raħ	yijo	keno raħ	yijo
Niħna	xam	niji	raħ	niji	kinna raħ	niji

Notes
This verb is unique in its structure and conjugation. There is no other verb that resembles it in the whole of the Lebanese language. It is considered an irregular verb.

Yufi

Group: 4Ba

To keep a promise | To repay a debt

Principal Forms

Pronoun	Infinitive	Simple Present	Perfect Present	Simple Past	Imperative
Ana	ufi	bufi	wefi	wafayt	
Inta	tufi	btufi	wefi	wafayt	wfii
Inti	tufi	btufi	wefyi	wafayti	wfii
Into	tufo	btufo	wefyiin	wafayto	wfu
Huwwi	yufi	byufi	wefi	wafa	
Hiyyi	tufi	btufi	wefyi	wafit	
Hinni	yufo	byufo	wefyiin	wafo	
Niħna	nufi	mnufi	wefyiin	wafayna	

Past Tense Forms

Pronoun + To Be		Past Continuous		Past Habit	Past Perfect	Past Anterior
Ana	kint	xam	ufi	ufi	wefi	wafayt
Inta	kint	xam	tufi	tufi	wefi	wafayt
Inti	kinti	xam	tufi	tufi	wefyi	wafayti
Into	kinto	xam	tufo	tufo	wefyiin	wafayto
Huwwi	ken	xam	yufi	yufi	wefi	wafa
Hiyyi	kenit	xam	tufi	tufi	wefyi	wafit
Hinni	keno	xam	yufo	yufo	wefyiin	wafo
Niħna	kinna	xam	nufi	nufi	wefyiin	wafayna

Present and Future Tense Forms

Pronoun	Present Continuous		Simple Future		Anterior Future	
Ana	xam	ufi	raħ	ufi	kint raħ	ufi
Inta	xam	tufi	raħ	tufi	kint raħ	tufi
Inti	xam	tufi	raħ	tufi	kinti raħ	tufi
Into	xam	tufo	raħ	tufo	kinto raħ	tufo
Huwwi	xam	yufi	raħ	yufi	ken raħ	yufi
Hiyyi	xam	tufi	raħ	tufi	kenit raħ	tufi
Hinni	xam	yufo	raħ	yufo	keno raħ	yufo
Niħna	xam	nufi	raħ	nufi	kinna raħ	nufi

Notes
This verb is the first of two forms of verbs that belong to the same group. These two verb forms are identical in conjugation except in the simple past tense and its dependant forms.

Yumi

To insinuate

Group: 4Bb

Principal Forms

Pronoun	Infinitive	Simple Present	Perfect Present	Simple Past	Imperative
Ana	umi	bumi	wemi	wmiit	
Inta	tumi	btumi	wemi	wmiit	wmii
Inti	tumi	btumi	wemyi	wmiiti	wmii
Into	tumo	btumo	wemyiin	wmiito	wmu
Huwwi	yumi	byumi	wemi	wimi	
Hiyyi	tumi	btumi	wemyi	wimyit	
Hinni	yumo	byumo	wemyiin	wimyo	
Niħna	numi	mnumi	wemyiin	wmiina	

Past Tense Forms

Pronoun + To Be		Past Continuous		Past Habit	Past Perfect	Past Anterior
Ana	kint	xam	umi	umi	wemi	wmiit
Inta	kint	xam	tumi	tumi	wemi	wmiit
Inti	kinti	xam	tumi	tumi	wemyi	wmiiti
Into	kinto	xam	tumo	tumo	wemyiin	wmiito
Huwwi	ken	xam	yumi	yumi	wemi	wimi
Hiyyi	kenit	xam	tumi	tumi	wemyi	wimyit
Hinni	keno	xam	yumo	yumo	wemyiin	wimyo
Niħna	kinna	xam	numi	numi	wemyiin	wmiina

Present and Future Tense Forms

Pronoun	Present Continuous		Simple Future		Anterior Future	
Ana	xam	umi	raħ	umi	kint raħ	umi
Inta	xam	tumi	raħ	tumi	kint raħ	tumi
Inti	xam	tumi	raħ	tumi	kinti raħ	tumi
Into	xam	tumo	raħ	tumo	kinto raħ	tumo
Huwwi	xam	yumi	raħ	yumi	ken raħ	yumi
Hiyyi	xam	tumi	raħ	tumi	kenit raħ	tumi
Hinni	xam	yumo	raħ	yumo	keno raħ	yumo
Niħna	xam	numi	raħ	numi	kinna raħ	numi

Notes
This verb is the second form of conjugation in group 4B. It is similar to the first form except in the simple past principal form and the verb forms dependant on the simple past tense.

Yuxa

To wake up

Group: 4C

Principal Forms

Pronoun	Infinitive	Simple Present	Perfect Present	Simple Past	Imperative
Ana	uxa	buxa	wexi	wxiit	
Inta	tuxa	btuxa	wexi	wxiit	wxaa
Inti	tuxi	btuxi	wexyi	wxiiti	wxii
Into	tuxo	btuxo	wexyiin	wxiito	wxu
Huwwi	yuxa	byuxa	wexi	wixi	
Hiyyi	tuxa	btuxa	wexyi	wixyit	
Hinni	yuxo	byuxo	wexyiin	wixyo	
Niħna	nuxa	mnuxa	wexyiin	wxiina	

Past Tense Forms

Pronoun + To Be		Past Continuous		Past Habit	Past Perfect	Past Anterior
Ana	**kint**	xam	uxa	uxa	wexi	wxiit
Inta	**kint**	xam	tuxa	tuxa	wexi	wxiit
Inti	**kinti**	xam	tuxi	tuxi	wexyi	wxiiti
Into	**kinto**	xam	tuxo	tuxo	wexyiin	wxiito
Huwwi	**ken**	xam	yuxa	yuxa	wexi	wixi
Hiyyi	**kenit**	xam	tuxa	tuxa	wexyi	wixyit
Hinni	**keno**	xam	yuxo	yuxo	wexyiin	wixyo
Niħna	**kinna**	xam	nuxa	nuxa	wexyiin	wxiina

Present and Future Tense Forms

Pronoun	Present Continuous		Simple Future		Anterior Future	
Ana	xam	uxa	raħ	uxa	kint raħ	uxa
Inta	xam	tuxa	raħ	tuxa	kint raħ	tuxa
Inti	xam	tuxi	raħ	tuxi	kinti raħ	tuxi
Into	xam	tuxo	raħ	tuxo	kinto raħ	tuxo
Huwwi	xam	yuxa	raħ	yuxa	ken raħ	yuxa
Hiyyi	xam	tuxa	raħ	tuxa	kenit raħ	tuxa
Hinni	xam	yuxo	raħ	yuxo	keno raħ	yuxo
Niħna	xam	nuxa	raħ	nuxa	kinna raħ	nuxa

Notes

This verb is characterized by the vowel "u" after the initial infinitive "y".

Ynem

To sleep

Group: 4D

Principal Forms

Pronoun	Infinitive	Simple Present	Perfect Present	Simple Past	Imperative
Ana	nem	bnem	neyim	nimit	
Inta	tnem	bitnem	neyim	nimit	nem
Inti	tnemi	bitnemi	neymi	nimti	nemi
Into	tnemo	bitnemo	neymiin	nimto	nemo
Huwwi	ynem	binem	neyim	nem	
Hiyyi	tnem	bitnem	neymi	nemit	
Hinni	ynemo	binemo	neymiin	nemo	
Niħna	nnem	minnem	neymiin	nimna	

Past Tense Forms

Pronoun + To Be		Past Continuous		Past Habit	Past Perfect	Past Anterior
Ana	kint	xam	nem	nem	neyim	nimit
Inta	kint	xam	tnem	tnem	neyim	nimit
Inti	kinti	xam	tnemi	tnemi	neymi	nimti
Into	kinto	xam	tnemo	tnemo	neymiin	nimto
Huwwi	ken	xam	ynem	ynem	neyim	nem
Hiyyi	kenit	xam	tnem	tnem	neymi	nemit
Hinni	keno	xam	ynemo	ynemo	neymiin	nemo
Niħna	kinna	xam	nnem	nnem	neymiin	nimna

Present and Future Tense Forms

Pronoun	Present Continuous		Simple Future		Anterior Future	
Ana	xam	nem	raħ	nem	kint raħ	nem
Inta	xam	tnem	raħ	tnem	kint raħ	tnem
Inti	xam	tnemi	raħ	tnemi	kinti raħ	tnemi
Into	xam	tnemo	raħ	tnemo	kinto raħ	tnemo
Huwwi	xam	ynem	raħ	ynem	ken raħ	ynem
Hiyyi	xam	tnem	raħ	tnem	kenit raħ	tnem
Hinni	xam	ynemo	raħ	ynemo	keno raħ	ynemo
Niħna	xam	nnem	raħ	nnem	kinna raħ	nnem

Notes
Note that some accents in Lebanon substitute the vowel "e" in many cases with the long vowels "aa". In this case, you may hear someone pronouncing "ynem" as "ynaam".

Ydub

To melt

Group: 4Ea

Principal Forms

Pronoun	Infinitive	Simple Present	Perfect Present	Simple Past	Imperative
Ana	dub	bdub	deyib	dibt	
Inta	tdub	bitdub	deyib	dibt	dub
Inti	tdubi	bitdubi	deybi	dibti	dubi
Into	tdubo	bitdubo	deybiin	dibto	dubo
Huwwi	ydub	bidub	deyib	deb	
Hiyyi	tdub	bitdub	deybi	debit	
Hinni	ydubo	bidubo	deybiin	debo	
Niħna	ndub	mindub	deybiin	dibna	

Past Tense Forms

Pronoun + To Be		Past Continuous		Past Habit	Past Perfect	Past Anterior
Ana	kint	xam	dub	dub	deyib	dibt
Inta	kint	xam	tdub	tdub	deyib	dibt
Inti	kinti	xam	tdubi	tdubi	deybi	dibti
Into	kinto	xam	tdubo	tdubo	deybiin	dibto
Huwwi	ken	xam	ydub	ydub	deyib	deb
Hiyyi	kenit	xam	tdub	tdub	deybi	debit
Hinni	keno	xam	ydubo	ydubo	deybiin	debo
Niħna	kinna	xam	ndub	ndub	deybiin	dibna

Present and Future Tense Forms

Pronoun	Present Continuous		Simple Future		Anterior Future	
Ana	xam	dub	raħ	dub	kint raħ	dub
Inta	xam	tdub	raħ	tdub	kint raħ	tdub
Inti	xam	tdubi	raħ	tdubi	kinti raħ	tdubi
Into	xam	tdubo	raħ	tdubo	kinto raħ	tdubo
Huwwi	xam	ydub	raħ	ydub	ken raħ	ydub
Hiyyi	xam	tdub	raħ	tdub	kenit raħ	tdub
Hinni	xam	ydubo	raħ	ydubo	keno raħ	ydubo
Niħna	xam	ndub	raħ	ndub	kinna raħ	ndub

Notes

This verb is the first of two forms of verbs that belong to the same group. These two verb forms are identical in conjugation except that the second form starts with an aleph.

Y`ul

To say

Group: 4Eb

Principal Forms

Pronoun	Infinitive	Simple Present	Perfect Present	Simple Past	Imperative
Ana	ul	b`ul	eyil	ilt	
Inta	t`ul	bit`ul	eyil	ilt	ul
Inti	t`uli	bit`uli	eyli	ilti	uli
Into	t`ulo	bit`ulo	eyliin	ilto	ulo
Huwwi	y`ul	bi`ul	eyil	el	
Hiyyi	t`ul	bit`ul	eyli	elit	
Hinni	y`ulo	bi`ulo	eyliin	elo	
Niħna	n`ul	min`ul	eyliin	ilna	

Past Tense Forms

Pronoun + To Be		Past Continuous		Past Habit	Past Perfect	Past Anterior
Ana	**kint**	xam	ul	ul	eyil	ilt
Inta	**kint**	xam	t`ul	t`ul	eyil	ilt
Inti	**kinti**	xam	t`uli	t`uli	eyli	ilti
Into	**kinto**	xam	t`ulo	t`ulo	eyliin	ilto
Huwwi	**ken**	xam	y`ul	y`ul	eyil	el
Hiyyi	**kenit**	xam	t`ul	t`ul	eyli	elit
Hinni	**keno**	xam	y`ulo	y`ulo	eyliin	elo
Niħna	**kinna**	xam	n`ul	n`ul	eyliin	ilna

Present and Future Tense Forms

Pronoun	Present Continuous		Simple Future		Anterior Future	
Ana	xam	ul	raħ	ul	kint raħ	ul
Inta	xam	t`ul	raħ	t`ul	kint raħ	t`ul
Inti	xam	t`uli	raħ	t`uli	kinti raħ	t`uli
Into	xam	t`ulo	raħ	t`ulo	kinto raħ	t`ulo
Huwwi	xam	y`ul	raħ	y`ul	ken raħ	y`ul
Hiyyi	xam	t`ul	raħ	t`ul	kenit raħ	t`ul
Hinni	xam	y`ulo	raħ	y`ulo	keno raħ	y`ulo
Niħna	xam	n`ul	raħ	n`ul	kinna raħ	n`ul

Notes

The aleph sound before a vowel in the verb is not written down in the beginning of the word because the vowel expresses the sound ` without a need to write it.

Yzur

To visit

Group: 4F

Principal Forms

Pronoun	Infinitive	Simple Present	Perfect Present	Simple Past	Imperative
Ana	zur	bzur	zeyir	zirt	
Inta	tzur	bitzur	zeyr	zirt	zur
Inti	tzuri	bitzuri	zeyri	zirti	zuri
Into	tzuro	bitzuro	zeyriin	zirto	zuro
Huwwi	yzur	bizur	zeyir	zaar	
Hiyyi	tzur	bitzur	zeyri	zaarit	
Hinni	yzuro	bizuro	zeyriin	zaaro	
Niħna	nzur	minzur	zeyriin	zirna	

Past Tense Forms

Pronoun + To Be		Past Continuous		Past Habit	Past Perfect	Past Anterior
Ana	**kint**	xam	zur	zur	zeyir	zirt
Inta	**kint**	xam	tzur	tzur	zeyr	zirt
Inti	**kinti**	xam	tzuri	tzuri	zeyri	zirti
Into	**kinto**	xam	tzuro	tzuro	zeyriin	zirto
Huwwi	**ken**	xam	yzur	yzur	zeyir	zaar
Hiyyi	**kenit**	xam	tzur	tzur	zeyri	zaarit
Hinni	**keno**	xam	yzuro	yzuro	zeyriin	zaaro
Niħna	**kinna**	xam	nzur	nzur	zeyriin	zirna

Present and Future Tense Forms

Pronoun	Present Continuous		Simple Future		Anterior Future	
Ana	xam	zur	raħ	zur	kint raħ	zur
Inta	xam	tzur	raħ	tzur	kint raħ	tzur
Inti	xam	tzuri	raħ	tzuri	kinti raħ	tzuri
Into	xam	tzuro	raħ	tzuro	kinto raħ	tzuro
Huwwi	xam	yzur	raħ	yzur	ken raħ	yzur
Hiyyi	xam	tzur	raħ	tzur	kenit raħ	tzur
Hinni	xam	yzuro	raħ	yzuro	keno raħ	yzuro
Niħna	xam	nzur	raħ	nzur	kinna raħ	nzur

Notes
The distinctive feature of this verb is the vowel "u" before the last letter in the infinitive form.

Yaxṫi

To give

Group: 5A

Principal Forms

Pronoun	Infinitive	Simple Present	Perfect Present	Simple Past	Imperative
Ana	axṫi	baxṫi	xaaṫi	xaṫayt	
Inta	taxṫi	btaxṫi	xaaṫi	xaṫayt	xṫii
Inti	taxṫi	btaxṫi	xaaṫyi	xaṫayti	xṫii
Into	taxṫo	btaxṫo	xaaṫyiin	xaṫayto	xṫu
Huwwi	yaxṫi	byaxṫi	xaaṫi	xaṫa	
Hiyyi	taxṫi	btaxṫi	xaaṫyi	xaṫit	
Hinni	yaxṫo	byaxṫo	xaaṫyiin	xaṫo	
Niħna	naxṫi	mnaxṫi	xaaṫyiin	xaṫayna	

Past Tense Forms

Pronoun + To Be		Past Continuous		Past Habit	Past Perfect	Past Anterior
Ana	**kint**	xam	axṫi	axṫi	xaaṫi	xaṫayt
Inta	**kint**	xam	taxṫi	taxṫi	xaaṫi	xaṫayt
Inti	**kinti**	xam	taxṫi	taxṫi	xaaṫyi	xaṫayti
Into	**kinto**	xam	taxṫo	taxṫo	xaaṫyiin	xaṫayto
Huwwi	**ken**	xam	yaxṫi	yaxṫi	xaaṫi	xaṫa
Hiyyi	**kenit**	xam	taxṫi	taxṫi	xaaṫyi	xaṫit
Hinni	**keno**	xam	yaxṫo	yaxṫo	xaaṫyiin	xaṫo
Niħna	**kinna**	xam	naxṫi	naxṫi	xaaṫyiin	xaṫayna

Present and Future Tense Forms

Pronoun	Present Continuous		Simple Future		Anterior Future	
Ana	xam	axṫi	raħ	axṫi	kint raħ	axṫi
Inta	xam	taxṫi	raħ	taxṫi	kint raħ	taxṫi
Inti	xam	taxṫi	raħ	taxṫi	kinti raħ	taxṫi
Into	xam	taxṫo	raħ	taxṫo	kinto raħ	taxṫo
Huwwi	xam	yaxṫi	raħ	yaxṫi	ken raħ	yaxṫi
Hiyyi	xam	taxṫi	raħ	taxṫi	kenit raħ	taxṫi
Hinni	xam	yaxṫo	raħ	yaxṫo	keno raħ	yaxṫo
Niħna	xam	naxṫi	raħ	naxṫi	kinna raħ	naxṫi

Notes

This form is a very unique verb form. It is in a group by itself. It is similar to Group 5Fa except in the Perfrcy Present Tense.

Yekol

To eat

Group: 5B

Principal Forms

Pronoun	Infinitive	Simple Present	Perfect Present	Simple Past	Imperative
Ana	ekol	bekol	ekil	akalt	
Inta	tekol	btekol	ekil	akalt	kul
Inti	tekli	btekli	ekli	akalti	kili
Into	teklo	bteklo	ekliin	akalto	kilo
Huwwi	yekol	byekol	ekil	akal	
Hiyyi	tekol	btekol	ekli	akalit	
Hinni	yeklo	byeklo	ekliin	akalo	
Niħna	nekol	mnekol	ekliin	akalna	

Past Tense Forms

Pronoun + To Be		Past Continuous		Past Habit	Past Perfect	Past Anterior
Ana	kint	xam	ekol	ekol	ekil	akalt
Inta	kint	xam	tekol	tekol	ekil	akalt
Inti	kinti	xam	tekli	tekli	ekli	akalti
Into	kinto	xam	teklo	teklo	ekliin	akalto
Huwwi	ken	xam	yekol	yekol	ekil	akal
Hiyyi	kenit	xam	tekol	tekol	ekli	akalit
Hinni	keno	xam	yeklo	yeklo	ekliin	akalo
Niħna	kinna	xam	nekol	nekol	ekliin	akalna

Present and Future Tense Forms

Pronoun	Present Continuous		Simple Future		Anterior Future	
Ana	xam	ekol	raħ	ekol	kint raħ	ekol
Inta	xam	tekol	raħ	tekol	kint raħ	tekol
Inti	xam	tekli	raħ	tekli	kinti raħ	tekli
Into	xam	teklo	raħ	teklo	kinto raħ	teklo
Huwwi	xam	yekol	raħ	yekol	ken raħ	yekol
Hiyyi	xam	tekol	raħ	tekol	kenit raħ	tekol
Hinni	xam	yeklo	raħ	yeklo	keno raħ	yeklo
Niħna	xam	nekol	raħ	nekol	kinna raħ	nekol

Notes

There aren't many Lebanese verbs that belong to this group. In this book there is only one other verb in this group which is verb "yeḱod" which means "to take".

Yimci

To walk

Group: 5C

Principal Forms

Pronoun	Infinitive	Simple Present	Perfect Present	Simple Past	Imperative
Ana	imci	bimci	meci	mciit	
Inta	timci	btimci	meci	mciit	mcii
Inti	timci	btimci	mecyi	mciiti	mcii
Into	timco	btimco	mecyiin	mciito	mcu
Huwwi	yimci	byimci	meci	mici	
Hiyyi	timci	btimci	mecyi	micyit	
Hinni	yimco	byimco	mecyiin	micyo	
Niħna	nimci	mnimci	mecyiin	mciina	

Past Tense Forms

Pronoun + To Be		Past Continuous		Past Habit	Past Perfect	Past Anterior
Ana	**kint**	xam	imci	imci	meci	mciit
Inta	**kint**	xam	timci	timci	meci	mciit
Inti	**kinti**	xam	timci	timci	mecyi	mciiti
Into	**kinto**	xam	timco	timco	mecyiin	mciito
Huwwi	**ken**	xam	yimci	yimci	meci	mici
Hiyyi	**kenit**	xam	timci	timci	mecyi	micyit
Hinni	**keno**	xam	yimco	yimco	mecyiin	micyo
Niħna	**kinna**	xam	nimci	nimci	mecyiin	mciina

Present and Future Tense Forms

Pronoun	Present Continuous		Simple Future		Anterior Future	
Ana	xam	imci	raħ	imci	kint raħ	imci
Inta	xam	timci	raħ	timci	kint raħ	timci
Inti	xam	timci	raħ	timci	kinti raħ	timci
Into	xam	timco	raħ	timco	kinto raħ	timco
Huwwi	xam	yimci	raħ	yimci	ken raħ	yimci
Hiyyi	xam	timci	raħ	timci	kenit raħ	timci
Hinni	xam	yimco	raħ	yimco	keno raħ	yimco
Niħna	xam	nimci	raħ	nimci	kinna raħ	nimci

Notes

This verb, eventhough it shares similarities with group 5Da, it differs in the conjugation of its past tense prinicipal forms.

Yirmi

To throw

Group: 5Da

Principal Forms

Pronoun	Infinitive	Simple Present	Perfect Present	Simple Past	Imperative
Ana	irmi	birmi	remi	ramayt	
Inta	tirmi	btirmi	remi	ramayt	rmii
Inti	tirmi	btirmi	remyi	ramayti	rmii
Into	tirmo	btirmo	remyiin	ramayto	rmu
Huwwi	yirmi	byirmi	remi	rama	
Hiyyi	tirmi	btirmi	remyi	ramit	
Hinni	yirmo	byirmo	remyiin	ramo	
Niħna	nirmi	mnirmi	remyiin	ramayna	

Past Tense Forms

Pronoun + To Be		Past Continuous		Past Habit	Past Perfect	Past Anterior
Ana	**kint**	xam	irmi	irmi	remi	ramayt
Inta	**kint**	xam	tirmi	tirmi	remi	ramayt
Inti	**kinti**	xam	tirmi	tirmi	remyi	ramayti
Into	**kinto**	xam	tirmo	tirmo	remyiin	ramayto
Huwwi	**ken**	xam	yirmi	yirmi	remi	rama
Hiyyi	**kenit**	xam	tirmi	tirmi	remyi	ramit
Hinni	**keno**	xam	yirmo	yirmo	remyiin	ramo
Niħna	**kinna**	xam	nirmi	nirmi	remyiin	ramayna

Present and Future Tense Forms

Pronoun	Present Continuous		Simple Future		Anterior Future	
Ana	xam	irmi	raħ	irmi	kint raħ	irmi
Inta	xam	tirmi	raħ	tirmi	kint raħ	tirmi
Inti	xam	tirmi	raħ	tirmi	kinti raħ	tirmi
Into	xam	tirmo	raħ	tirmo	kinto raħ	tirmo
Huwwi	xam	yirmi	raħ	yirmi	ken raħ	yirmi
Hiyyi	xam	tirmi	raħ	tirmi	kenit raħ	tirmi
Hinni	xam	yirmo	raħ	yirmo	keno raħ	yirmo
Niħna	xam	nirmi	raħ	nirmi	kinna raħ	nirmi

Notes
This is a fairly common verb form in the Lebanese language.

Yi`li

To fry

Group: 5Db

Principal Forms

Pronoun	Infinitive	Simple Present	Perfect Present	Simple Past	Imperative
Ana	i`li	bi`li	eli	alayt	
Inta	ti`li	bti`li	eli	alayt	`lii
Inti	ti`li	bti`li	elyi	alayti	`lii
Into	ti`lo	bti`lo	elyiin	alayto	`lu
Huwwi	yi`li	byi`li	eli	ala	
Hiyyi	ti`li	bti`li	elyi	alit	
Hinni	yi`lo	byi`lo	elyiin	alo	
Niħna	ni`li	mni`li	elyiin	alayna	

Past Tense Forms

Pronoun + To Be		Past Continuous		Past Habit	Past Perfect	Past Anterior
Ana	kint	xam	i`li	i`li	eli	alayt
Inta	kint	xam	ti`li	ti`li	eli	alayt
Inti	kinti	xam	ti`li	ti`li	elyi	alayti
Into	kinto	xam	ti`lo	ti`lo	elyiin	alayto
Huwwi	ken	xam	yi`li	yi`li	eli	ala
Hiyyi	kenit	xam	ti`li	ti`li	elyi	alit
Hinni	keno	xam	yi`lo	yi`lo	elyiin	alo
Niħna	kinna	xam	ni`li	ni`li	elyiin	alayna

Present and Future Tense Forms

Pronoun	Present Continuous		Simple Future		Anterior Future	
Ana	xam	i`li	raħ	i`li	kint raħ	i`li
Inta	xam	ti`li	raħ	ti`li	kint raħ	ti`li
Inti	xam	ti`li	raħ	ti`li	kinti raħ	ti`li
Into	xam	ti`lo	raħ	ti`lo	kinto raħ	ti`lo
Huwwi	xam	yi`li	raħ	yi`li	ken raħ	yi`li
Hiyyi	xam	ti`li	raħ	ti`li	kenit raħ	ti`li
Hinni	xam	yi`lo	raħ	yi`lo	keno raħ	yi`lo
Niħna	xam	ni`li	raħ	ni`li	kinna raħ	ni`li

Notes

The aleph sound before a vowel in the verb is not written down in the beginning of the word because the vowel expresses the sound ` without a need to write it.

Yinsa

To forget

Group: 5Ea

Principal Forms

Pronoun	Infinitive	Simple Present	Perfect Present	Simple Past	Imperative
Ana	insa	binsa	nesi	nsiit	
Inta	tinsa	btinsa	nesi	nsiit	nsaa
Inti	tinsi	btinsi	nesyi	nsiiti	nsii
Into	tinso	btinso	nesyiin	nsiito	nsu
Huwwi	yinsa	byinsa	nesi	nisi	
Hiyyi	tinsa	btinsa	nesyi	nisyit	
Hinni	yinso	byinso	nesyiin	nisyo	
Niħna	ninsa	mninsa	nesyiin	nsiina	

Past Tense Forms

Pronoun + To Be		Past Continuous		Past Habit	Past Perfect	Past Anterior
Ana	kint	xam	insa	insa	nesi	nsiit
Inta	kint	xam	tinsa	tinsa	nesi	nsiit
Inti	kinti	xam	tinsi	tinsi	nesyi	nsiiti
Into	kinto	xam	tinso	tinso	nesyiin	nsiito
Huwwi	ken	xam	yinsa	yinsa	nesi	nisi
Hiyyi	kenit	xam	tinsa	tinsa	nesyi	nisyit
Hinni	keno	xam	yinso	yinso	nesyiin	nisyo
Niħna	kinna	xam	ninsa	ninsa	nesyiin	nsiina

Present and Future Tense Forms

Pronoun	Present Continuous		Simple Future		Anterior Future	
Ana	xam	insa	raħ	insa	kint raħ	insa
Inta	xam	tinsa	raħ	tinsa	kint raħ	tinsa
Inti	xam	tinsi	raħ	tinsi	kinti raħ	tinsi
Into	xam	tinso	raħ	tinso	kinto raħ	tinso
Huwwi	xam	yinsa	raħ	yinsa	ken raħ	yinsa
Hiyyi	xam	tinsa	raħ	tinsa	kenit raħ	tinsa
Hinni	xam	yinso	raħ	yinso	keno raħ	yinso
Niħna	xam	ninsa	raħ	ninsa	kinna raħ	ninsa

Notes
This form is similar to form 5D except in the conjugation of the past tenses.

Yi`sa

To harden

Group: 5Eb

Principal Forms

Pronoun	Infinitive	Simple Present	Perfect Present	Simple Past	Imperative
Ana	i`sa	bi`sa	esi	`siit	
Inta	ti`sa	bti`sa	esi	`siit	`saa
Inti	ti`si	bti`si	esyi	`siiti	`sii
Into	ti`so	bti`so	esyiin	`siito	`su
Huwwi	yi`sa	byi`sa	esi	isi	
Hiyyi	ti`sa	bti`sa	esyi	isyit	
Hinni	yi`so	byi`so	esyiin	isyo	
Niħna	ni`sa	mni`sa	esyiin	`siina	

Past Tense Forms

Pronoun + To Be		Past Continuous		Past Habit	Past Perfect	Past Anterior
Ana	kint	xam	i`sa	i`sa	esi	`siit
Inta	kint	xam	ti`sa	ti`sa	esi	`siit
Inti	kinti	xam	ti`si	ti`si	esyi	`siiti
Into	kinto	xam	ti`so	ti`so	esyiin	`siito
Huwwi	ken	xam	yi`sa	yi`sa	esi	isi
Hiyyi	kenit	xam	ti`sa	ti`sa	esyi	isyit
Hinni	keno	xam	yi`so	yi`so	esyiin	isyo
Niħna	kinna	xam	ni`sa	ni`sa	esyiin	`siina

Present and Future Tense Forms

Pronoun	Present Continuous		Simple Future		Anterior Future	
Ana	xam	i`sa	raħ	i`sa	kint raħ	i`sa
Inta	xam	ti`sa	raħ	ti`sa	kint raħ	ti`sa
Inti	xam	ti`si	raħ	ti`si	kinti raħ	ti`si
Into	xam	ti`so	raħ	ti`so	kinto raħ	ti`so
Huwwi	xam	yi`sa	raħ	yi`sa	ken raħ	yi`sa
Hiyyi	xam	ti`sa	raħ	ti`sa	kenit raħ	ti`sa
Hinni	xam	yi`so	raħ	yi`so	keno raħ	yi`so
Niħna	xam	ni`sa	raħ	ni`sa	kinna raħ	ni`sa

Notes

This form is almost identical to group 5Ea except that the Perfect Present tense does not express the aleph sound in it spelling.

Yoṫfi

To turn off

Group: 5Fa

Principal Forms

Pronoun	Infinitive	Simple Present	Perfect Present	Simple Past	Imperative
Ana	oṫfi	boṫfi	ṫaafi	ṫafayt	
Inta	toṫfi	btoṫfi	ṫaafi	ṫafayt	ṫfii
Inti	toṫfi	btoṫfi	ṫaafyi	ṫafayti	ṫfii
Into	toṫfo	btoṫfo	ṫaafyiin	ṫafayto	ṫfu
Huwwi	yoṫfi	byoṫfi	ṫaafi	ṫafa	
Hiyyi	toṫfi	btoṫfi	ṫaafyi	ṫafit	
Hinni	yoṫfo	byoṫfo	ṫaafyiin	ṫafo	
Niħna	noṫfi	mnoṫfi	ṫaafyiin	ṫafayna	

Past Tense Forms

Pronoun + To Be		Past Continuous		Past Habit	Past Perfect	Past Anterior
Ana	**kint**	xam	oṫfi	oṫfi	ṫaafi	ṫafayt
Inta	**kint**	xam	toṫfi	toṫfi	ṫaafi	ṫafayt
Inti	**kinti**	xam	toṫfi	toṫfi	ṫaafyi	ṫafayti
Into	**kinto**	xam	toṫfo	toṫfo	ṫaafyiin	ṫafayto
Huwwi	**ken**	xam	yoṫfi	yoṫfi	ṫaafi	ṫafa
Hiyyi	**kenit**	xam	toṫfi	toṫfi	ṫaafyi	ṫafit
Hinni	**keno**	xam	yoṫfo	yoṫfo	ṫaafyiin	ṫafo
Niħna	**kinna**	xam	noṫfi	noṫfi	ṫaafyiin	ṫafayna

Present and Future Tense Forms

Pronoun	Present Continuous		Simple Future		Anterior Future	
Ana	xam	oṫfi	raħ	oṫfi	kint raħ	oṫfi
Inta	xam	toṫfi	raħ	toṫfi	kint raħ	toṫfi
Inti	xam	toṫfi	raħ	toṫfi	kinti raħ	toṫfi
Into	xam	toṫfo	raħ	toṫfo	kinto raħ	toṫfo
Huwwi	xam	yoṫfi	raħ	yoṫfi	ken raħ	yoṫfi
Hiyyi	xam	toṫfi	raħ	toṫfi	kenit raħ	toṫfi
Hinni	xam	yoṫfo	raħ	yoṫfo	keno raħ	yoṫfo
Niħna	xam	noṫfi	raħ	noṫfi	kinna raħ	noṫfi

Notes

Note that some accents in Lebanon use the "o" sound expressed in this verb form and other accents use an "i" instead. In this respect, this form could be compared with form 5Da.

Yorḋi

To please

Group: 5Fb

Principal Forms

Pronoun	Infinitive	Simple Present	Perfect Present	Simple Past	Imperative
Ana	orḋi	borḋi	raaḋi	rḋiit	
Inta	torḋi	btorḋi	raaḋi	rḋiit	rḋaa
Inti	torḋi	btorḋi	raaḋyi	rḋiiti	rḋii
Into	torḋo	btorḋo	raaḋyiin	rḋiito	rḋu
Huwwi	yorḋi	byorḋi	raaḋi	roḋi	
Hiyyi	torḋi	btorḋi	raaḋyi	roḋyit	
Hinni	yorḋo	byorḋo	raaḋyiin	roḋyo	
Niḣna	norḋi	mnorḋi	raaḋyiin	rḋiina	

Past Tense Forms

Pronoun + To Be		Past Continuous		Past Habit	Past Perfect	Past Anterior
Ana	**kint**	xam	orḋi	orḋi	raaḋi	rḋiit
Inta	**kint**	xam	torḋi	torḋi	raaḋi	rḋiit
Inti	**kinti**	xam	torḋi	torḋi	raaḋyi	rḋiiti
Into	**kinto**	xam	torḋo	torḋo	raaḋyiin	rḋiito
Huwwi	**ken**	xam	yorḋi	yorḋi	raaḋi	roḋi
Hiyyi	**kenit**	xam	torḋi	torḋi	raaḋyi	roḋyit
Hinni	**keno**	xam	yorḋo	yorḋo	raaḋyiin	roḋyo
Niḣna	**kinna**	xam	norḋi	norḋi	raaḋyiin	rḋiina

Present and Future Tense Forms

Pronoun	Present Continuous		Simple Future		Anterior Future	
Ana	xam	orḋi	raḣ	orḋi	kint raḣ	orḋi
Inta	xam	torḋi	raḣ	torḋi	kint raḣ	torḋi
Inti	xam	torḋi	raḣ	torḋi	kinti raḣ	torḋi
Into	xam	torḋo	raḣ	torḋo	kinto raḣ	torḋo
Huwwi	xam	yorḋi	raḣ	yorḋi	ken raḣ	yorḋi
Hiyyi	xam	torḋi	raḣ	torḋi	kenit raḣ	torḋi
Hinni	xam	yorḋo	raḣ	yorḋo	keno raḣ	yorḋo
Niḣna	xam	norḋi	raḣ	norḋi	kinna raḣ	norḋi

Notes

This group is almost identical to group 5Fa except in the conjugation of the Simple Past Tense and the Imperative tense.

Ycimm

To smell

Group: 5Ga

Principal Forms

Pronoun	Infinitive	Simple Present	Perfect Present	Simple Past	Imperative
Ana	cimm	bcimm	cemim	cammayt	
Inta	tcimm	bitcimm	cemim	cammayt	cimm
Inti	tcimmi	bitcimmi	cemmi	cammayti	cimmi
Into	tcimmo	bitcimmo	cemmiin	cammayto	cimmo
Huwwi	ycimm	bicimm	cemim	camm	
Hiyyi	tcimm	bitcimm	cemmi	cammit	
Hinni	ycimmo	bicimmo	cemmiin	cammo	
Niħna	ncimm	mincimm	cemmiin	cammayna	

Past Tense Forms

Pronoun + To Be		Past Continuous		Past Habit	Past Perfect	Past Anterior
Ana	kint	xam	cimm	cimm	cemim	cammayt
Inta	kint	xam	tcimm	tcimm	cemim	cammayt
Inti	kinti	xam	tcimmi	tcimmi	cemmi	cammayti
Into	kinto	xam	tcimmo	tcimmo	cemmiin	cammayto
Huwwi	ken	xam	ycimm	ycimm	cemim	camm
Hiyyi	kenit	xam	tcimm	tcimm	cemmi	cammit
Hinni	keno	xam	ycimmo	ycimmo	cemmiin	cammo
Niħna	kinna	xam	ncimm	ncimm	cemmiin	cammayna

Present and Future Tense Forms

Pronoun	Present Continuous		Simple Future		Anterior Future	
Ana	xam	cimm	raħ	cimm	kint raħ	cimm
Inta	xam	tcimm	raħ	tcimm	kint raħ	tcimm
Inti	xam	tcimmi	raħ	tcimmi	kinti raħ	tcimmi
Into	xam	tcimmo	raħ	tcimmo	kinto raħ	tcimmo
Huwwi	xam	ycimm	raħ	ycimm	ken raħ	ycimm
Hiyyi	xam	tcimm	raħ	tcimm	kenit raħ	tcimm
Hinni	xam	ycimmo	raħ	ycimmo	keno raħ	ycimmo
Niħna	xam	ncimm	raħ	ncimm	kinna raħ	ncimm

Notes
This tense is characterized by the double consonant at the end of the infinitive for of the verb.

Y`iħħ

To cough

Group: 5Gb

Principal Forms

Pronoun	Infinitive	Simple Present	Perfect Present	Simple Past	Imperative
Ana	iħħ	b`iħħ	eħiħ	aħħayt	
Inta	t`iħħ	bit`iħħ	eħiħ	aħħayt	iħħ
Inti	t`iħħi	bit`iħħi	eħħa	aħħayti	iħħi
Into	t`iħħo	bit`iħħo	eħħiin	aħħayto	iħħo
Huwwi	y`iħħ	bi`iħħ	eħiħ	aħħ	
Hiyyi	t`iħħ	bit`iħħ	eħħa	aħħit	
Hinni	y`iħħo	bi`iħħo	eħħiin	aħħo	
Niħna	n`iħħ	min`iħħ	eħħiin	aħħayna	

Past Tense Forms

Pronoun + To Be		Past Continuous		Past Habit	Past Perfect	Past Anterior
Ana	**kint**	xam	iħħ	iħħ	eħiħ	aħħayt
Inta	**kint**	xam	t`iħħ	t`iħħ	eħiħ	aħħayt
Inti	**kinti**	xam	t`iħħi	t`iħħi	eħħa	aħħayti
Into	**kinto**	xam	t`iħħo	t`iħħo	eħħiin	aħħayto
Huwwi	**ken**	xam	y`iħħ	y`iħħ	eħiħ	aħħ
Hiyyi	**kenit**	xam	t`iħħ	t`iħħ	eħħa	aħħit
Hinni	**keno**	xam	y`iħħo	y`iħħo	eħħiin	aħħo
Niħna	**kinna**	xam	n`iħħ	n`iħħ	eħħiin	aħħayna

Present and Future Tense Forms

Pronoun	Present Continuous		Simple Future		Anterior Future	
Ana	xam	iħħ	raħ	iħħ	kint raħ	iħħ
Inta	xam	t`iħħ	raħ	t`iħħ	kint raħ	t`iħħ
Inti	xam	t`iħħi	raħ	t`iħħi	kinti raħ	t`iħħi
Into	xam	t`iħħo	raħ	t`iħħo	kinto raħ	t`iħħo
Huwwi	xam	y`iħħ	raħ	y`iħħ	ken raħ	y`iħħ
Hiyyi	xam	t`iħħ	raħ	t`iħħ	kenit raħ	t`iħħ
Hinni	xam	y`iħħo	raħ	y`iħħo	keno raħ	y`iħħo
Niħna	xam	n`iħħ	raħ	n`iħħ	kinna raħ	n`iħħ

Notes

The aleph sound before a vowel in the verb is not written down in the beginning of the word because the vowel expresses the sound ` without a need to write it.

Yxaḋḋ

To bite

Group: 5Gc

Principal Forms

Pronoun	Infinitive	Simple Present	Perfect Present	Simple Past	Imperative
Ana	xaḋḋ	bxaḋḋ	xaadiḋ	xaḋḋayt	
Inta	txaḋḋ	bitxaḋḋ	xaadiḋ	xaḋḋayt	xaḋḋ
Inti	txaḋḋi	bitxaḋḋi	xaaḋḋa	xaḋḋayti	xaḋḋi
Into	txaḋḋo	bitxaḋḋo	xaaḋḋiin	xaḋḋayto	xaḋḋo
Huwwi	yxaḋḋ	bixaḋḋ	xaadiḋ	xaḋḋ	
Hiyyi	txaḋḋ	bitxaḋḋ	xaaḋḋa	xaḋḋit	
Hinni	yxaḋḋo	bixaḋḋo	xaaḋḋiin	xaḋḋo	
Niħna	nxaḋḋ	minxaḋḋ	xaaḋḋiin	xaḋḋayna	

Past Tense Forms

Pronoun + To Be		Past Continuous		Past Habit	Past Perfect	Past Anterior
Ana	kint	xam	xaḋḋ	xaḋḋ	xaadiḋ	xaḋḋayt
Inta	kint	xam	txaḋḋ	txaḋḋ	xaadiḋ	xaḋḋayt
Inti	kinti	xam	txaḋḋi	txaḋḋi	xaaḋḋa	xaḋḋayti
Into	kinto	xam	txaḋḋo	txaḋḋo	xaaḋḋiin	xaḋḋayto
Huwwi	ken	xam	yxaḋḋ	yxaḋḋ	xaadiḋ	xaḋḋ
Hiyyi	kenit	xam	txaḋḋ	txaḋḋ	xaaḋḋa	xaḋḋit
Hinni	keno	xam	yxaḋḋo	yxaḋḋo	xaaḋḋiin	xaḋḋo
Niħna	kinna	xam	nxaḋḋ	nxaḋḋ	xaaḋḋiin	xaḋḋayna

Present and Future Tense Forms

Pronoun	Present Continuous		Simple Future		Anterior Future	
Ana	xam	xaḋḋ	raħ	xaḋḋ	kint raħ	xaḋḋ
Inta	xam	txaḋḋ	raħ	txaḋḋ	kint raħ	txaḋḋ
Inti	xam	txaḋḋi	raħ	txaḋḋi	kinti raħ	txaḋḋi
Into	xam	txaḋḋo	raħ	txaḋḋo	kinto raħ	txaḋḋo
Huwwi	xam	yxaḋḋ	raħ	yxaḋḋ	ken raħ	yxaḋḋ
Hiyyi	xam	txaḋḋ	raħ	txaḋḋ	kenit raħ	txaḋḋ
Hinni	xam	yxaḋḋo	raħ	yxaḋḋo	keno raħ	yxaḋḋo
Niħna	xam	nxaḋḋ	raħ	nxaḋḋ	kinna raħ	nxaḋḋ

Notes

This group is part of group 5G because even though the vowels are different in these two groups, the conjugation rules are exactly the same.

Yjiib

To bring

Group: 5Ha

Principal Forms

Pronoun	Infinitive	Simple Present	Perfect Present	Simple Past	Imperative
Ana	jiib	bjiib	jeyib	jibt	
Inta	tjiib	bitjiib	jeyib	jibt	jiib
Inti	tjiibi	bitjiibi	jeybi	jibti	jiibi
Into	tjiibo	bitjiibo	jeybiin	jibto	jiibo
Huwwi	yjiib	bijiib	jeyib	jeb	
Hiyyi	tjiib	bitjiib	jeybi	jebit	
Hinni	yjiibo	bijiibo	jeybiin	jebo	
Niħna	njiib	minjiib	jeybiin	jibna	

Past Tense Forms

Pronoun + To Be		Past Continuous		Past Habit	Past Perfect	Past Anterior
Ana	**kint**	xam	jiib	jiib	jeyib	jibt
Inta	**kint**	xam	tjiib	tjiib	jeyib	jibt
Inti	**kinti**	xam	tjiibi	tjiibi	jeybi	jibti
Into	**kinto**	xam	tjiibo	tjiibo	jeybiin	jibto
Huwwi	**ken**	xam	yjiib	yjiib	jeyib	jeb
Hiyyi	**kenit**	xam	tjiib	tjiib	jeybi	jebit
Hinni	**keno**	xam	yjiibo	yjiibo	jeybiin	jebo
Niħna	**kinna**	xam	njiib	njiib	jeybiin	jibna

Present and Future Tense Forms

Pronoun	Present Continuous		Simple Future		Anterior Future	
Ana	xam	jiib	raħ	jiib	kint raħ	jiib
Inta	xam	tjiib	raħ	tjiib	kint raħ	tjiib
Inti	xam	tjiibi	raħ	tjiibi	kinti raħ	tjiibi
Into	xam	tjiibo	raħ	tjiibo	kinto raħ	tjiibo
Huwwi	xam	yjiib	raħ	yjiib	ken raħ	yjiib
Hiyyi	xam	tjiib	raħ	tjiib	kenit raħ	tjiib
Hinni	xam	yjiibo	raħ	yjiibo	keno raħ	yjiibo
Niħna	xam	njiib	raħ	njiib	kinna raħ	njiib

Notes
The defining vowels in this group are the double "ii" in the infinitive form.

Yṡiir

To become

Group: 5Hb

Principal Forms

Pronoun	Infinitive	Simple Present	Perfect Present	Simple Past	Imperative
Ana	ṡiir	bṡiir	ṡaayir	ṡort	
Inta	tṡiir	bitṡiir	ṡaayir	ṡort	ṡiir
Inti	tṡiiri	bitṡiiri	ṡaayra	ṡorti	ṡiiri
Into	tṡiiro	bitṡiiro	ṡaayriin	ṡorto	ṡiiro
Huwwi	yṡiir	biṡiir	ṡaayir	ṡaar	
Hiyyi	tṡiir	bitṡiir	ṡaayra	ṡaarit	
Hinni	yṡiiro	biṡiiro	ṡaayriin	ṡaaro	
Niħna	nṡiir	minṡiir	ṡaayriin	ṡorna	

Past Tense Forms

Pronoun + To Be		Past Continuous		Past Habit	Past Perfect	Past Anterior
Ana	kint	xam	ṡiir	ṡiir	ṡaayir	ṡort
Inta	kint	xam	tṡiir	tṡiir	ṡaayir	ṡort
Inti	kinti	xam	tṡiiri	tṡiiri	ṡaayra	ṡorti
Into	kinto	xam	tṡiiro	tṡiiro	ṡaayriin	ṡorto
Huwwi	ken	xam	yṡiir	yṡiir	ṡaayir	ṡaar
Hiyyi	kenit	xam	tṡiir	tṡiir	ṡaayra	ṡaarit
Hinni	keno	xam	yṡiiro	yṡiiro	ṡaayriin	ṡaaro
Niħna	kinna	xam	nṡiir	nṡiir	ṡaayriin	ṡorna

Present and Future Tense Forms

Pronoun	Present Continuous		Simple Future		Anterior Future	
Ana	xam	ṡiir	raħ	ṡiir	kint raħ	ṡiir
Inta	xam	tṡiir	raħ	tṡiir	kint raħ	tṡiir
Inti	xam	tṡiiri	raħ	tṡiiri	kinti raħ	tṡiiri
Into	xam	tṡiiro	raħ	tṡiiro	kinto raħ	tṡiiro
Huwwi	xam	yṡiir	raħ	yṡiir	ken raħ	yṡiir
Hiyyi	xam	tṡiir	raħ	tṡiir	kenit raħ	tṡiir
Hinni	xam	yṡiiro	raħ	yṡiiro	keno raħ	yṡiiro
Niħna	xam	nṡiir	raħ	nṡiir	kinna raħ	nṡiir

Notes
This group is almost the same as the previous group except that the "e" sound is replaced with the "aa" sound in the Perfect Present, and the "i" is replaced with the "o" in the simple past.

Yṡobb

To pour

Group: 5la

Principal Forms

Pronoun	Infinitive	Simple Present	Perfect Present	Simple Past	Imperative
Ana	ṡobb	bṡobb	ṡaabib	ṡabbayt	
Inta	tṡobb	bitṡobb	ṡaabib	ṡabbayt	ṡobb
Inti	tṡobbi	bitṡobbi	ṡaabbi	ṡabbayti	ṡobbi
Into	tṡobbo	bitṡobbo	ṡaabbiin	ṡabbayto	ṡobbo
Huwwi	yṡobb	biṡobb	ṡaabib	ṡabb	
Hiyyi	tṡobb	bitṡobb	ṡaabbi	ṡabbit	
Hinni	yṡobbo	biṡobbo	ṡaabbiin	ṡabbo	
Niħna	nṡobb	minṡobb	ṡaabbiin	ṡabbayna	

Past Tense Forms

Pronoun + To Be		Past Continuous		Past Habit	Past Perfect	Past Anterior
Ana	kint	xam	ṡobb	ṡobb	ṡaabib	ṡabbayt
Inta	kint	xam	tṡobb	tṡobb	ṡaabib	ṡabbayt
Inti	kinti	xam	tṡobb	tṡobb	ṡaabbi	ṡabbayti
Into	kinto	xam	tṡobb	tṡobb	ṡaabbiin	ṡabbayto
Huwwi	ken	xam	yṡobb	yṡobb	ṡaabib	ṡabb
Hiyyi	kenit	xam	tṡobb	tṡobb	ṡaabbi	ṡabbit
Hinni	keno	xam	yṡobb	yṡobb	ṡaabbiin	ṡabbo
Niħna	kinna	xam	nṡobb	nṡobb	ṡaabbiin	ṡabbayna

Present and Future Tense Forms

Pronoun	Present Continuous		Simple Future		Anterior Future	
Ana	xam	ṡobb	raħ	ṡobb	kint raħ	ṡobb
Inta	xam	tṡobb	raħ	tṡobb	kint raħ	tṡobb
Inti	xam	tṡobb	raħ	tṡobb	kinti raħ	tṡobb
Into	xam	tṡobb	raħ	tṡobb	kinto raħ	tṡobb
Huwwi	xam	yṡobb	raħ	yṡobb	ken raħ	yṡobb
Hiyyi	xam	tṡobb	raħ	tṡobb	kenit raħ	tṡobb
Hinni	xam	yṡobb	raħ	yṡobb	keno raħ	yṡobb
Niħna	xam	nṡobb	raħ	nṡobb	kinna raħ	nṡobb

Notes

The verbs in this group are distinguished by the "o" vowel and the double consonant at the end of the verb.

Y`oṡṡ

To cut

Group: 5Ib

Principal Forms

Pronoun	Infinitive	Simple Present	Perfect Present	Simple Past	Imperative
Ana	oṡṡ	b`oṡṡ	aaṡiṡ	aṡṡayt	
Inta	t`oṡṡ	bit`oṡṡ	aaṡiṡ	aṡṡayt	oṡṡ
Inti	t`oṡṡi	bit`oṡṡi	aaṡṡa	aṡṡayti	oṡṡi
Into	t`oṡṡo	bit`oṡṡo	aaṡṡiin	aṡṡayto	oṡṡo
Huwwi	y`oṡṡ	bi`oṡṡ	aaṡiṡ	aṡṡ	
Hiyyi	t`oṡṡ	bit`oṡṡ	aaṡṡa	aṡṡit	
Hinni	y`oṡṡo	bi`oṡṡo	aaṡṡiin	aṡṡo	
Niħna	n`oṡṡ	min`oṡṡ	aaṡṡiin	aṡṡayna	

Past Tense Forms

Pronoun + To Be		Past Continuous		Past Habit	Past Perfect	Past Anterior
Ana	kint	xam	oṡṡ	oṡṡ	aaṡiṡ	aṡṡayt
Inta	kint	xam	t`oṡṡ	t`oṡṡ	aaṡiṡ	aṡṡayt
Inti	kinti	xam	t`oṡṡ	t`oṡṡ	aaṡṡa	aṡṡayti
Into	kinto	xam	t`oṡṡ	t`oṡṡ	aaṡṡiin	aṡṡayto
Huwwi	ken	xam	y`oṡṡ	y`oṡṡ	aaṡiṡ	aṡṡ
Hiyyi	kenit	xam	t`oṡṡ	t`oṡṡ	aaṡṡa	aṡṡit
Hinni	keno	xam	y`oṡṡ	y`oṡṡ	aaṡṡiin	aṡṡo
Niħna	kinna	xam	n`oṡṡ	n`oṡṡ	aaṡṡiin	aṡṡayna

Present and Future Tense Forms

Pronoun	Present Continuous		Simple Future		Anterior Future	
Ana	xam	oṡṡ	raħ	oṡṡ	kint raħ	oṡṡ
Inta	xam	t`oṡṡ	raħ	t`oṡṡ	kint raħ	t`oṡṡ
Inti	xam	t`oṡṡ	raħ	t`oṡṡ	kinti raħ	t`oṡṡ
Into	xam	t`oṡṡ	raħ	t`oṡṡ	kinto raħ	t`oṡṡ
Huwwi	xam	y`oṡṡ	raħ	y`oṡṡ	ken raħ	y`oṡṡ
Hiyyi	xam	t`oṡṡ	raħ	t`oṡṡ	kenit raħ	t`oṡṡ
Hinni	xam	y`oṡṡ	raħ	y`oṡṡ	keno raħ	y`oṡṡ
Niħna	xam	n`oṡṡ	raħ	n`oṡṡ	kinna raħ	n`oṡṡ

Notes

The aleph sound before a vowel in the verb is not written down in the beginning of the word because the vowel expresses the sound ` without a need to write it.

Yu`af

To stand

Group: 5Ja

Principal Forms

Pronoun	Infinitive	Simple Present	Perfect Present	Simple Past	Imperative
Ana	u`af	bu`af	we`if	w`ift	
Inta	tu`af	btu`af	we`if	w`ift	w`aaf
Inti	tu`afi	btu`afi	we`fi	w`ifti	w`afi
Into	tu`afo	btu`afo	we`fiin	w`ifto	w`afo
Huwwi	yu`af	byu`af	we`if	wi`if	
Hiyyi	tu`af	btu`af	we`fi	wi`fit	
Hinni	yu`afo	byu`afo	we`fiin	wi`fo	
Niħna	nu`af	mnu`af	we`fiin	w`ifna	

Past Tense Forms

Pronoun + To Be		Past Continuous		Past Habit	Past Perfect	Past Anterior
Ana	**kint**	xam	u`af	u`af	we`if	w`ift
Inta	**kint**	xam	tu`af	tu`af	we`if	w`ift
Inti	**kinti**	xam	tu`afi	tu`afi	we`fi	w`ifti
Into	**kinto**	xam	tu`afo	tu`afo	we`fiin	w`ifto
Huwwi	**ken**	xam	yu`af	yu`af	we`if	wi`if
Hiyyi	**kenit**	xam	tu`af	tu`af	we`fi	wi`fit
Hinni	**keno**	xam	yu`afo	yu`afo	we`fiin	wi`fo
Niħna	**kinna**	xam	nu`af	nu`af	we`fiin	w`ifna

Present and Future Tense Forms

Pronoun	Present Continuous		Simple Future		Anterior Future	
Ana	xam	u`af	raħ	u`af	kint raħ	u`af
Inta	xam	tu`af	raħ	tu`af	kint raħ	tu`af
Inti	xam	tu`afi	raħ	tu`afi	kinti raħ	tu`afi
Into	xam	tu`afo	raħ	tu`afo	kinto raħ	tu`afo
Huwwi	xam	yu`af	raħ	yu`af	ken raħ	yu`af
Hiyyi	xam	tu`af	raħ	tu`af	kenit raħ	tu`af
Hinni	xam	yu`afo	raħ	yu`afo	keno raħ	yu`afo
Niħna	xam	nu`af	raħ	nu`af	kinna raħ	nu`af

Notes

The verbs in this group are characterized by the “u” vowel after the infinitive “y”.

Yuxod

To promise

Group: 5Jb

Principal Forms

Pronoun	Infinitive	Simple Present	Perfect Present	Simple Past	Imperative
Ana	uxod	buxod	wexid	waxadt	
Inta	tuxod	btuxod	wexid	waxadt	wxud
Inti	tuxdi	btuxdi	wexdi	waxadti	wxidi
Into	tuxdo	btuxdo	wexdiin	waxadto	wxido
Huwwi	yuxod	byuxod	wexid	waxad	
Hiyyi	tuxod	btuxod	wexdi	waxadit	
Hinni	yuxdo	byuxdo	wexdiin	waxado	
Niħna	nuxod	mnuxod	wexdiin	waxadna	

Past Tense Forms

Pronoun + To Be		Past Continuous		Past Habit	Past Perfect	Past Anterior
Ana	kint	xam	uxod	uxod	wexid	waxadt
Inta	kint	xam	tuxod	tuxod	wexid	waxadt
Inti	kinti	xam	tuxdi	tuxdi	wexdi	waxadti
Into	kinto	xam	tuxdo	tuxdo	wexdiin	waxadto
Huwwi	ken	xam	yuxod	yuxod	wexid	waxad
Hiyyi	kenit	xam	tuxod	tuxod	wexdi	waxadit
Hinni	keno	xam	yuxdo	yuxdo	wexdiin	waxado
Niħna	kinna	xam	nuxod	nuxod	wexdiin	waxadna

Present and Future Tense Forms

Pronoun	Present Continuous		Simple Future		Anterior Future	
Ana	xam	uxod	raħ	uxod	kint raħ	uxod
Inta	xam	tuxod	raħ	tuxod	kint raħ	tuxod
Inti	xam	tuxdi	raħ	tuxdi	kinti raħ	tuxdi
Into	xam	tuxdo	raħ	tuxdo	kinto raħ	tuxdo
Huwwi	xam	yuxod	raħ	yuxod	ken raħ	yuxod
Hiyyi	xam	tuxod	raħ	tuxod	kenit raħ	tuxod
Hinni	xam	yuxdo	raħ	yuxdo	keno raħ	yuxdo
Niħna	xam	nuxod	raħ	nuxod	kinna raħ	nuxod

Notes

This group has a different conjugation for the Simple Past tense than the previous group, otherwise everything else is similar.

Ynedi

Group: 5K

To call | To shout for someone

Principal Forms

Pronoun	Infinitive	Simple Present	Perfect Present	Simple Past	Imperative
Ana	nedi	bnedi	mnedi	nedayt	
Inta	tnedi	bitnedi	mnedi	nedayt	nedi
Inti	tnedi	bitnedi	mnedyi	nedayti	nedi
Into	tnedo	bitnedo	mnedyiin	nedayto	nedo
Huwwi	ynedi	binedi	mnedi	neda	
Hiyyi	tnedi	bitnedi	mnedyi	nedit	
Hinni	ynedo	binedo	mnedyiin	nedo	
Niħna	nnedi	minnedi	mnedyiin	nedayna	

Past Tense Forms

Pronoun + To Be		Past Continuous		Past Habit	Past Perfect	Past Anterior
Ana	kint	xam	nedi	nedi	mnedi	nedayt
Inta	kint	xam	tnedi	tnedi	mnedi	nedayt
Inti	kinti	xam	tnedi	tnedi	mnedyi	nedayti
Into	kinto	xam	tnedo	tnedo	mnedyiin	nedayto
Huwwi	ken	xam	ynedi	ynedi	mnedi	neda
Hiyyi	kenit	xam	tnedi	tnedi	mnedyi	nedit
Hinni	keno	xam	ynedo	ynedo	mnedyiin	nedo
Niħna	kinna	xam	nnedi	nnedi	mnedyiin	nedayna

Present and Future Tense Forms

Pronoun	Present Continuous		Simple Future		Anterior Future	
Ana	xam	nedi	raħ	nedi	kint raħ	nedi
Inta	xam	tnedi	raħ	tnedi	kint raħ	tnedi
Inti	xam	tnedi	raħ	tnedi	kinti raħ	tnedi
Into	xam	tnedo	raħ	tnedo	kinto raħ	tnedo
Huwwi	xam	ynedi	raħ	ynedi	ken raħ	ynedi
Hiyyi	xam	tnedi	raħ	tnedi	kenit raħ	tnedi
Hinni	xam	ynedo	raħ	ynedo	keno raħ	ynedo
Niħna	xam	nnedi	raħ	nnedi	kinna raħ	nnedi

Notes
This is not a very common verb group. It is characterized by the middle vowel "e".

Yaxmil

To do

Group: 6A

Principal Forms

Pronoun	Infinitive	Simple Present	Perfect Present	Simple Past	Imperative
Ana	axmil	baxmil	xemil	xmilt	
Inta	taxmil	btaxmil	xemil	xmilt	xmul
Inti	taximli	btaximli	xemli	xmilti	xmili
Into	taximlo	btaximlo	xemliin	xmilto	xmilo
Huwwi	yaxmil	byaxmil	xemil	ximil	
Hiyyi	taxmil	btaxmil	xemli	ximlit	
Hinni	yaximlo	byaximlo	xemliin	ximlo	
Niħna	naxmil	mnaxmil	xemliin	xmilna	

Past Tense Forms

Pronoun + To Be		Past Continuous		Past Habit	Past Perfect	Past Anterior
Ana	**kint**	xam	axmil	axmil	xemil	xmilt
Inta	**kint**	xam	taxmil	taxmil	xemil	xmilt
Inti	**kinti**	xam	taximli	taximli	xemli	xmilti
Into	**kinto**	xam	taximlo	taximlo	xemliin	xmilto
Huwwi	**ken**	xam	yaxmil	yaxmil	xemil	ximil
Hiyyi	**kenit**	xam	taxmil	taxmil	xemli	ximlit
Hinni	**keno**	xam	yaximlo	yaximlo	xemliin	ximlo
Niħna	**kinna**	xam	naxmil	naxmil	xemliin	xmilna

Present and Future Tense Forms

Pronoun	Present Continuous		Simple Future		Anterior Future	
Ana	xam	axmil	raħ	axmil	kint raħ	axmil
Inta	xam	taxmil	raħ	taxmil	kint raħ	taxmil
Inti	xam	taximli	raħ	taximli	kinti raħ	taximli
Into	xam	taximlo	raħ	taximlo	kinto raħ	taximlo
Huwwi	xam	yaxmil	raħ	yaxmil	ken raħ	yaxmil
Hiyyi	xam	taxmil	raħ	taxmil	kenit raħ	taxmil
Hinni	xam	yaximlo	raħ	yaximlo	keno raħ	yaximlo
Niħna	xam	naxmil	raħ	naxmil	kinna raħ	naxmil

Notes
The only other verb in this book that belongs to this group is "yaxrif" which means "to know".

Yidhan

To paint

Group: 6Ba

Principal Forms

Pronoun	Infinitive	Simple Present	Perfect Present	Simple Past	Imperative
Ana	idhan	bidhan	dehin	dahant	
Inta	tidhan	btidhan	dehin	dahant	dhaan
Inti	tidhani	btidhani	dehni	dahanti	dhani
Into	tidhano	btidhano	dehniin	dahanto	dhano
Huwwi	yidhan	byidhan	dehin	dahan	
Hiyyi	tidhan	btidhan	dehni	dahanit	
Hinni	yidhano	byidhano	dehniin	dahano	
Niħna	nidhan	mnidhan	dehniin	dahanna	

Past Tense Forms

Pronoun + To Be		Past Continuous		Past Habit	Past Perfect	Past Anterior
Ana	**kint**	xam	idhan	idhan	dehin	dahant
Inta	**kint**	xam	tidhan	tidhan	dehin	dahant
Inti	**kinti**	xam	tidhani	tidhani	dehni	dahanti
Into	**kinto**	xam	tidhano	tidhano	dehniin	dahanto
Huwwi	**ken**	xam	yidhan	yidhan	dehin	dahan
Hiyyi	**kenit**	xam	tidhan	tidhan	dehni	dahanit
Hinni	**keno**	xam	yidhano	yidhano	dehniin	dahano
Niħna	**kinna**	xam	nidhan	nidhan	dehniin	dahanna

Present and Future Tense Forms

Pronoun	Present Continuous		Simple Future		Anterior Future	
Ana	xam	idhan	raħ	idhan	kint raħ	idhan
Inta	xam	tidhan	raħ	tidhan	kint raħ	tidhan
Inti	xam	tidhani	raħ	tidhani	kinti raħ	tidhani
Into	xam	tidhano	raħ	tidhano	kinto raħ	tidhano
Huwwi	xam	yidhan	raħ	yidhan	ken raħ	yidhan
Hiyyi	xam	tidhan	raħ	tidhan	kenit raħ	tidhan
Hinni	xam	yidhano	raħ	yidhano	keno raħ	yidhano
Niħna	xam	nidhan	raħ	nidhan	kinna raħ	nidhan

Notes
This is a very common verb group in the Lebanese language.

Yi`daħ

To drill

Group: 6Bb

Principal Forms

Pronoun	Infinitive	Simple Present	Perfect Present	Simple Past	Imperative
Ana	i`daħ	bi`daħ	ediħ	adaħt	
Inta	ti`daħ	bti`daħ	ediħ	adaħt	`daaħ
Inti	ti`daħi	bti`daħi	edħa	adaħti	`daħi
Into	ti`daħo	bti`daħo	edħiin	adaħto	`daħo
Huwwi	yi`daħ	byi`daħ	ediħ	adaħ	
Hiyyi	ti`daħ	bti`daħ	edħa	adaħit	
Hinni	yi`daħo	byi`daħo	edħiin	adaħo	
Niħna	ni`daħ	mni`daħ	edħiin	adaħna	

Past Tense Forms

Pronoun + To Be		Past Continuous		Past Habit	Past Perfect	Past Anterior
Ana	kint	xam	i`daħ	i`daħ	ediħ	adaħt
Inta	kint	xam	ti`daħ	ti`daħ	ediħ	adaħt
Inti	kinti	xam	ti`daħi	ti`daħi	edħa	adaħti
Into	kinto	xam	ti`daħo	ti`daħo	edħiin	adaħto
Huwwi	ken	xam	yi`daħ	yi`daħ	ediħ	adaħ
Hiyyi	kenit	xam	ti`daħ	ti`daħ	edħa	adaħit
Hinni	keno	xam	yi`daħo	yi`daħo	edħiin	adaħo
Niħna	kinna	xam	ni`daħ	ni`daħ	edħiin	adaħna

Present and Future Tense Forms

Pronoun	Present Continuous		Simple Future		Anterior Future	
Ana	xam	i`daħ	raħ	i`daħ	kint raħ	i`daħ
Inta	xam	ti`daħ	raħ	ti`daħ	kint raħ	ti`daħ
Inti	xam	ti`daħi	raħ	ti`daħi	kinti raħ	ti`daħi
Into	xam	ti`daħo	raħ	ti`daħo	kinto raħ	ti`daħo
Huwwi	xam	yi`daħ	raħ	yi`daħ	ken raħ	yi`daħ
Hiyyi	xam	ti`daħ	raħ	ti`daħ	kenit raħ	ti`daħ
Hinni	xam	yi`daħo	raħ	yi`daħo	keno raħ	yi`daħo
Niħna	xam	ni`daħ	raħ	ni`daħ	kinna raħ	ni`daħ

Notes
The aleph sound before a vowel in the verb is not written down in the beginning of the Present Perfect and Simple Past because the vowel expresses the sound ` without a need to write it.

Yożrax

To plant

Group: 6Bc

Principal Forms

Pronoun	Infinitive	Simple Present	Perfect Present	Simple Past	Imperative
Ana	ożrax	bożrax	żaarix	żaraxt	
Inta	tożrax	btożrax	żaarix	żaraxt	żraax
Inti	tożraxi	btożraxi	żaarxa	żaraxti	żraxi
Into	tożraxo	btożraxo	żaarxiin	żaraxto	żraxo
Huwwi	yożrax	byożrax	żaarix	żarax	
Hiyyi	tożrax	btożrax	żaarxa	żaraxit	
Hinni	yożraxo	byożraxo	żaarxiin	żaraxo	
Niħna	nożrax	mnożrax	żaarxiin	żaraxna	

Past Tense Forms

Pronoun + To Be		Past Continuous		Past Habit	Past Perfect	Past Anterior
Ana	kint	xam	ożrax	ożrax	żaarix	żaraxt
Inta	kint	xam	tożrax	tożrax	żaarix	żaraxt
Inti	kinti	xam	tożraxi	tożraxi	żaarxa	żaraxti
Into	kinto	xam	tożraxo	tożraxo	żaarxiin	żaraxto
Huwwi	ken	xam	yożrax	yożrax	żaarix	żarax
Hiyyi	kenit	xam	tożrax	tożrax	żaarxa	żaraxit
Hinni	keno	xam	yożraxo	yożraxo	żaarxiin	żaraxo
Niħna	kinna	xam	nożrax	nożrax	żaarxiin	żaraxna

Present and Future Tense Forms

Pronoun	Present Continuous		Simple Future		Anterior Future	
Ana	xam	ożrax	raħ	ożrax	kint raħ	ożrax
Inta	xam	tożrax	raħ	tożrax	kint raħ	tożrax
Inti	xam	tożraxi	raħ	tożraxi	kinti raħ	tożraxi
Into	xam	tożraxo	raħ	tożraxo	kinto raħ	tożraxo
Huwwi	xam	yożrax	raħ	yożrax	ken raħ	yożrax
Hiyyi	xam	tożrax	raħ	tożrax	kenit raħ	tożrax
Hinni	xam	yożraxo	raħ	yożraxo	keno raħ	yożraxo
Niħna	xam	nożrax	raħ	nożrax	kinna raħ	nożrax

Notes
Some Lebanese accents use the “o” sound, and some use instead the “i”. In this sense, this verb group could be compared to group 6Ba.

Yo`har

To tease

Group: 6Bd

Principal Forms

Pronoun	Infinitive	Simple Present	Perfect Present	Simple Past	Imperative
Ana	o`har	bo`har	aahir	ahart	
Inta	to`har	bto`har	aahir	ahart	`haar
Inti	to`hari	bto`hari	aahra	aharti	`hari
Into	to`haro	bto`haro	aahriin	aharto	`haro
Huwwi	yo`har	byo`har	aahir	ahar	
Hiyyi	to`har	bto`har	aahra	aharit	
Hinni	yo`haro	byo`haro	aahriin	aharo	
Niħna	no`har	mno`har	aahriin	aharna	

Past Tense Forms

Pronoun + To Be		Past Continuous		Past Habit	Past Perfect	Past Anterior
Ana	kint	xam	o`har	o`har	aahir	ahart
Inta	kint	xam	to`har	to`har	aahir	ahart
Inti	kinti	xam	to`hari	to`hari	aahra	aharti
Into	kinto	xam	to`haro	to`haro	aahriin	aharto
Huwwi	ken	xam	yo`har	yo`har	aahir	ahar
Hiyyi	kenit	xam	to`har	to`har	aahra	aharit
Hinni	keno	xam	yo`haro	yo`haro	aahriin	aharo
Niħna	kinna	xam	no`har	no`har	aahriin	aharna

Present and Future Tense Forms

Pronoun	Present Continuous		Simple Future		Anterior Future	
Ana	xam	o`har	raħ	o`har	kint raħ	o`har
Inta	xam	to`har	raħ	to`har	kint raħ	to`har
Inti	xam	to`hari	raħ	to`hari	kinti raħ	to`hari
Into	xam	to`haro	raħ	to`haro	kinto raħ	to`haro
Huwwi	xam	yo`har	raħ	yo`har	ken raħ	yo`har
Hiyyi	xam	to`har	raħ	to`har	kenit raħ	to`har
Hinni	xam	yo`haro	raħ	yo`haro	keno raħ	yo`haro
Niħna	xam	no`har	raħ	no`har	kinna raħ	no`har

Notes
The aleph sound before a vowel in the verb is not written down in the beginning of the Present Perfect and Simple Past because the vowel expresses the sound ` without a need to write it.

Yobrom

Group: 6Ca

To turn

Principal Forms

Pronoun	Infinitive	Simple Present	Perfect Present	Simple Past	Imperative
Ana	obrom	bobrom	baarim	baramt	
Inta	tobrom	btobrom	baarim	baramt	brum
Inti	tobormi	btobormi	baarmi	baramti	bromi
Into	tobormo	btobormo	baarmiin	baramto	bromo
Huwwi	yobrom	byobrom	baarim	baram	
Hiyyi	tobrom	btobrom	baarmi	baramit	
Hinni	yobormo	byobormo	baarmiin	baramo	
Niħna	nobrom	mnobrom	baarmiin	baramna	

Past Tense Forms

Pronoun + To Be		Past Continuous		Past Habit	Past Perfect	Past Anterior
Ana	kint	xam	obrom	obrom	baarim	baramt
Inta	kint	xam	tobrom	tobrom	baarim	baramt
Inti	kinti	xam	tobormi	tobormi	baarmi	baramti
Into	kinto	xam	tobormo	tobormo	baarmiin	baramto
Huwwi	ken	xam	yobrom	yobrom	baarim	baram
Hiyyi	kenit	xam	tobrom	tobrom	baarmi	baramit
Hinni	keno	xam	yobormo	yobormo	baarmiin	baramo
Niħna	kinna	xam	nobrom	nobrom	baarmiin	baramna

Present and Future Tense Forms

Pronoun	Present Continuous		Simple Future		Anterior Future	
Ana	xam	obrom	raħ	obrom	kint raħ	obrom
Inta	xam	tobrom	raħ	tobrom	kint raħ	tobrom
Inti	xam	tobormi	raħ	tobormi	kinti raħ	tobormi
Into	xam	tobormo	raħ	tobormo	kinto raħ	tobormo
Huwwi	xam	yobrom	raħ	yobrom	ken raħ	yobrom
Hiyyi	xam	tobrom	raħ	tobrom	kenit raħ	tobrom
Hinni	xam	yobormo	raħ	yobormo	keno raħ	yobormo
Niħna	xam	nobrom	raħ	nobrom	kinna raħ	nobrom

Notes
This verb group is characterized by the two “o” vowels.

Yo`mor

To command | To order

Group: 6Cb

Principal Forms

Pronoun	Infinitive	Simple Present	Perfect Present	Simple Past	Imperative
Ana	o`mor	bo`mor	aamir	amart	
Inta	to`mor	bto`mor	aamir	amart	`mur
Inti	to`omri	bto`omri	aamra	amarti	`mori
Into	to`omro	bto`omro	aamriin	amarto	`moro
Huwwi	yo`mor	byo`mor	aamir	amar	
Hiyyi	to`mor	bto`mor	aamra	amarit	
Hinni	yo`omro	byo`omro	aamriin	amaro	
Niħna	no`mor	mno`mor	aamriin	amarna	

Past Tense Forms

Pronoun + To Be		Past Continuous		Past Habit	Past Perfect	Past Anterior
Ana	**kint**	xam	o`mor	o`mor	aamir	amart
Inta	**kint**	xam	to`mor	to`mor	aamir	amart
Inti	**kinti**	xam	to`omri	to`omri	aamra	amarti
Into	**kinto**	xam	to`omro	to`omro	aamriin	amarto
Huwwi	**ken**	xam	yo`mor	yo`mor	aamir	amar
Hiyyi	**kenit**	xam	to`mor	to`mor	aamra	amarit
Hinni	**keno**	xam	yo`omro	yo`omro	aamriin	amaro
Niħna	**kinna**	xam	no`mor	no`mor	aamriin	amarna

Present and Future Tense Forms

Pronoun	Present Continuous		Simple Future		Anterior Future	
Ana	xam	o`mor	raħ	o`mor	kint raħ	o`mor
Inta	xam	to`mor	raħ	to`mor	kint raħ	to`mor
Inti	xam	to`omri	raħ	to`omri	kinti raħ	to`omri
Into	xam	to`omro	raħ	to`omro	kinto raħ	to`omro
Huwwi	xam	yo`mor	raħ	yo`mor	ken raħ	yo`mor
Hiyyi	xam	to`mor	raħ	to`mor	kenit raħ	to`mor
Hinni	xam	yo`omro	raħ	yo`omro	keno raħ	yo`omro
Niħna	xam	no`mor	raħ	no`mor	kinna raħ	no`mor

Notes

The aleph sound before a vowel in the verb is not written down in the beginning of the Present Perfect and Simple Past because the vowel expresses the sound ` without a need to write it.

Yhaddi

Group: 6Da

To hold

Principal Forms

Pronoun	Infinitive	Simple Present	Perfect Present	Simple Past	Imperative
Ana	haddi	bhaddi	mhaddi	haddayt	
Inta	thaddi	bithaddi	mhaddi	haddayt	haddi
Inti	thaddi	bithaddi	mhaddyyi	haddayti	haddi
Into	thaddo	bithaddo	mhaddyiin	haddayto	haddo
Huwwi	yhaddi	bihaddi	mhaddi	hadda	
Hiyyi	thaddi	bithaddi	mhaddyyi	haddit	
Hinni	yhaddo	bihaddo	mhaddyiin	haddo	
Niħna	nhaddi	minhaddi	mhaddyiin	haddayna	

Past Tense Forms

Pronoun + To Be		Past Continuous		Past Habit	Past Perfect	Past Anterior
Ana	**kint**	xam	haddi	haddi	mhaddi	haddayt
Inta	**kint**	xam	thaddi	thaddi	mhaddi	haddayt
Inti	**kinti**	xam	thaddi	thaddi	mhaddyyi	haddayti
Into	**kinto**	xam	thaddo	thaddo	mhaddyiin	haddayto
Huwwi	**ken**	xam	yhaddi	yhaddi	mhaddi	hadda
Hiyyi	**kenit**	xam	thaddi	thaddi	mhaddyyi	haddit
Hinni	**keno**	xam	yhaddo	yhaddo	mhaddyiin	haddo
Niħna	**kinna**	xam	nhaddi	nhaddi	mhaddyiin	haddayna

Present and Future Tense Forms

Pronoun	Present Continuous		Simple Future		Anterior Future	
Ana	xam	haddi	raħ	haddi	kint raħ	haddi
Inta	xam	thaddi	raħ	thaddi	kint raħ	thaddi
Inti	xam	thaddi	raħ	thaddi	kinti raħ	thaddi
Into	xam	thaddo	raħ	thaddo	kinto raħ	thaddo
Huwwi	xam	yhaddi	raħ	yhaddi	ken raħ	yhaddi
Hiyyi	xam	thaddi	raħ	thaddi	kenit raħ	thaddi
Hinni	xam	yhaddo	raħ	yhaddo	keno raħ	yhaddo
Niħna	xam	nhaddi	raħ	nhaddi	kinna raħ	nhaddi

Notes
This verb group is characterized by the double consonant before the last vowel in the infinitive.

Y`affi

To skip

Group: 6Db

Principal Forms

Pronoun	Infinitive	Simple Present	Perfect Present	Simple Past	Imperative
Ana	affi	b`affi	m`affi	affayt	
Inta	t`affi	bit`affi	m`affi	affayt	affi
Inti	t`affi	bit`affi	m`affyi	affayti	affi
Into	t`affo	bit`affo	m`affyiin	affayto	affo
Huwwi	y`affi	bi`affi	m`affi	affa	
Hiyyi	t`affi	bit`affi	m`affyi	affit	
Hinni	y`affo	bi`affo	m`affyiin	affo	
Niħna	n`affi	min`affi	m`affyiin	affayna	

Past Tense Forms

Pronoun + To Be		Past Continuous		Past Habit	Past Perfect	Past Anterior
Ana	kint	xam	affi	affi	m`affi	affayt
Inta	kint	xam	t`affi	t`affi	m`affi	affayt
Inti	kinti	xam	t`affi	t`affi	m`affyi	affayti
Into	kinto	xam	t`affo	t`affo	m`affyiin	affayto
Huwwi	ken	xam	y`affi	y`affi	m`affi	affa
Hiyyi	kenit	xam	t`affi	t`affi	m`affyi	affit
Hinni	keno	xam	y`affo	y`affo	m`affyiin	affo
Niħna	kinna	xam	n`affi	n`affi	m`affyiin	affayna

Present and Future Tense Forms

Pronoun	Present Continuous		Simple Future		Anterior Future	
Ana	xam	affi	raħ	affi	kint raħ	affi
Inta	xam	t`affi	raħ	t`affi	kint raħ	t`affi
Inti	xam	t`affi	raħ	t`affi	kinti raħ	t`affi
Into	xam	t`affo	raħ	t`affo	kinto raħ	t`affo
Huwwi	xam	y`affi	raħ	y`affi	ken raħ	y`affi
Hiyyi	xam	t`affi	raħ	t`affi	kenit raħ	t`affi
Hinni	xam	y`affo	raħ	y`affo	keno raħ	y`affo
Niħna	xam	n`affi	raħ	n`affi	kinna raħ	n`affi

Notes
The aleph sound before a vowel in the verb is not written down in the beginning of the Present Perfect and Simple Past because the vowel expresses the sound ` without a need to write it.

Yfarji

To show

Group: 6E

Principal Forms

Pronoun	Infinitive	Simple Present	Perfect Present	Simple Past	Imperative
Ana	farji	bfarji	mfarji	farjayt	
Inta	tfarji	bitfarji	mfarji	farjayt	farji
Inti	tfarji	bitfarji	mfarjyi	farjayti	farji
Into	tfarjo	bitfarjo	mfarjyiin	farjayto	farjo
Huwwi	yfarji	bifarji	mfarji	farja	
Hiyyi	tfarji	bitfarji	mfarjyi	farjit	
Hinni	yfarjo	bifarjo	mfarjyiin	farjo	
Niħna	nfarji	minnfarji	mfarjyiin	farjayna	

Past Tense Forms

Pronoun + To Be		Past Continuous		Past Habit	Past Perfect	Past Anterior
Ana	kint	xam	farji	farji	mfarji	farjayt
Inta	kint	xam	tfarji	tfarji	mfarji	farjayt
Inti	kinti	xam	tfarji	tfarji	mfarjyi	farjayti
Into	kinto	xam	tfarjo	tfarjo	mfarjyiin	farjayto
Huwwi	ken	xam	yfarji	yfarji	mfarji	farja
Hiyyi	kenit	xam	tfarji	tfarji	mfarjyi	farjit
Hinni	keno	xam	yfarjo	yfarjo	mfarjyiin	farjo
Niħna	kinna	xam	nfarji	nfarji	mfarjyiin	farjayna

Present and Future Tense Forms

Pronoun	Present Continuous		Simple Future		Anterior Future	
Ana	xam	farji	raħ	farji	kint raħ	farji
Inta	xam	tfarji	raħ	tfarji	kint raħ	tfarji
Inti	xam	tfarji	raħ	tfarji	kinti raħ	tfarji
Into	xam	tfarjo	raħ	tfarjo	kinto raħ	tfarjo
Huwwi	xam	yfarji	raħ	yfarji	ken raħ	yfarji
Hiyyi	xam	tfarji	raħ	tfarji	kenit raħ	tfarji
Hinni	xam	yfarjo	raħ	yfarjo	keno raħ	yfarjo
Niħna	xam	nfarji	raħ	nfarji	kinna raħ	nfarji

Notes
This is a fairly common verb group in the Lebanese language.

Yjewib

To answer

Group: 6F

Principal Forms

Pronoun	Infinitive	Simple Present	Perfect Present	Simple Past	Imperative
Ana	jewib	bjewib	mjewib	jewabt	
Inta	tjewib	bitjewib	mjewib	jewabt	jewib
Inti	tjewbi	bitjewbi	mjewbi	jewabti	jewbi
Into	tjewbo	bitjewbo	mjewbiin	jewabto	jewbo
Huwwi	yjewib	bijewib	mjewib	jewab	
Hiyyi	tjewib	bitjewib	mjewbi	jewabit	
Hinni	yjewbo	bijewbo	mjewbiin	jewabo	
Niħna	njewib	minjewib	mjewbiin	jewabna	

Past Tense Forms

Pronoun + To Be		Past Continuous		Past Habit	Past Perfect	Past Anterior
Ana	kint	xam	jewib	jewib	mjewib	jewabt
Inta	kint	xam	tjewib	tjewib	mjewib	jewabt
Inti	kinti	xam	tjewbi	tjewbi	mjewbi	jewabti
Into	kinto	xam	tjewbo	tjewbo	mjewbiin	jewabto
Huwwi	ken	xam	yjewib	yjewib	mjewib	jewab
Hiyyi	kenit	xam	tjewib	tjewib	mjewbi	jewabit
Hinni	keno	xam	yjewbo	yjewbo	mjewbiin	jewabo
Niħna	kinna	xam	njewib	njewib	mjewbiin	jewabna

Present and Future Tense Forms

Pronoun	Present Continuous		Simple Future		Anterior Future	
Ana	xam	jewib	raħ	jewib	kint raħ	jewib
Inta	xam	tjewib	raħ	tjewib	kint raħ	tjewib
Inti	xam	tjewbi	raħ	tjewbi	kinti raħ	tjewbi
Into	xam	tjewbo	raħ	tjewbo	kinto raħ	tjewbo
Huwwi	xam	yjewib	raħ	yjewib	ken raħ	yjewib
Hiyyi	xam	tjewib	raħ	tjewib	kenit raħ	tjewib
Hinni	xam	yjewbo	raħ	yjewbo	keno raħ	yjewbo
Niħna	xam	njewib	raħ	njewib	kinna raħ	njewib

Notes
This is a very common Lebanese verb form. It is useful to memorize the conjugations for this group by heart.

Yicrab

To drink

Group: 6Ga

Principal Forms

Pronoun	Infinitive	Simple Present	Perfect Present	Simple Past	Imperative
Ana	icrab	bicrab	cerib	cribt	
Inta	ticrab	bticrab	cerib	cribt	craab
Inti	ticrabi	bticrabi	cerbi	cribti	crabi
Into	ticrabo	bticrabo	cerbiin	cribto	crabo
Huwwi	yicrab	byicrab	cerib	cirib	
Hiyyi	ticrab	bticrab	cerbi	cirbit	
Hinni	yicrabo	byicrabo	cerbiin	cirbo	
Niħna	nicrab	mnicrab	cerbiin	cribna	

Past Tense Forms

Pronoun + To Be		Past Continuous		Past Habit	Past Perfect	Past Anterior
Ana	kint	xam	icrab	icrab	cerib	cribt
Inta	kint	xam	ticrab	ticrab	cerib	cribt
Inti	kinti	xam	ticrabi	ticrabi	cerbi	cribti
Into	kinto	xam	ticrabo	ticrabo	cerbiin	cribto
Huwwi	ken	xam	yicrab	yicrab	cerib	cirib
Hiyyi	kenit	xam	ticrab	ticrab	cerbi	cirbit
Hinni	keno	xam	yicrabo	yicrabo	cerbiin	cirbo
Niħna	kinna	xam	nicrab	nicrab	cerbiin	cribna

Present and Future Tense Forms

Pronoun	Present Continuous		Simple Future		Anterior Future	
Ana	xam	icrab	raħ	icrab	kint raħ	icrab
Inta	xam	ticrab	raħ	ticrab	kint raħ	ticrab
Inti	xam	ticrabi	raħ	ticrabi	kinti raħ	ticrabi
Into	xam	ticrabo	raħ	ticrabo	kinto raħ	ticrabo
Huwwi	xam	yicrab	raħ	yicrab	ken raħ	yicrab
Hiyyi	xam	ticrab	raħ	ticrab	kenit raħ	ticrab
Hinni	xam	yicrabo	raħ	yicrabo	keno raħ	yicrabo
Niħna	xam	nicrab	raħ	nicrab	kinna raħ	nicrab

Notes
This is also a fairly common verb group in the Lebanese language.

Yi`bal

To accept

Group: 6Gb

Principal Forms

Pronoun	Infinitive	Simple Present	Perfect Present	Simple Past	Imperative
Ana	i`bal	bi`bal	ebil	`bilt	
Inta	ti`bal	bti`bal	ebil	`bilt	`baal
Inti	ti`bali	bti`bali	ebli	`bilti	`bali
Into	ti`balo	bti`balo	ebliin	`bilto	`balo
Huwwi	yi`bal	byi`bal	ebil	ibil	
Hiyyi	ti`bal	bti`bal	ebli	iblit	
Hinni	yi`balo	byi`balo	ebliin	iblo	
Niħna	ni`bal	mni`bal	ebliin	`bilna	

Past Tense Forms

Pronoun + To Be		Past Continuous		Past Habit	Past Perfect	Past Anterior
Ana	kint	xam	i`bal	i`bal	ebil	`bilt
Inta	kint	xam	ti`bal	ti`bal	ebil	`bilt
Inti	kinti	xam	ti`bali	ti`bali	ebli	`bilti
Into	kinto	xam	ti`balo	ti`balo	ebliin	`bilto
Huwwi	ken	xam	yi`bal	yi`bal	ebil	ibil
Hiyyi	kenit	xam	ti`bal	ti`bal	ebli	iblit
Hinni	keno	xam	yi`balo	yi`balo	ebliin	iblo
Niħna	kinna	xam	ni`bal	ni`bal	ebliin	`bilna

Present and Future Tense Forms

Pronoun	Present Continuous		Simple Future		Anterior Future	
Ana	xam	i`bal	raħ	i`bal	kint raħ	i`bal
Inta	xam	ti`bal	raħ	ti`bal	kint raħ	ti`bal
Inti	xam	ti`bali	raħ	ti`bali	kinti raħ	ti`bali
Into	xam	ti`balo	raħ	ti`balo	kinto raħ	ti`balo
Huwwi	xam	yi`bal	raħ	yi`bal	ken raħ	yi`bal
Hiyyi	xam	ti`bal	raħ	ti`bal	kenit raħ	ti`bal
Hinni	xam	yi`balo	raħ	yi`balo	keno raħ	yi`balo
Niħna	xam	ni`bal	raħ	ni`bal	kinna raħ	ni`bal

Notes
The aleph sound before a vowel in the verb is not written down in the beginning of the Present Perfect and Simple Past because the vowel expresses the sound ` without a need to write it.

Yii`as

To lose hope

Group: 6H

Principal Forms

Pronoun	Infinitive	Simple Present	Perfect Present	Simple Past	Imperative
Ana	ii`as	bii`as	yi`sen	y`ist	
Inta	tii`as	btii`as	yi`sen	y`ist	y`aas
Inti	tii`asi	btii`asi	yi`seni	y`isti	y`asi
Into	tii`aso	btii`aso	yi`seniin	y`isto	y`aso
Huwwi	yii`as	byii`as	yi`sen	yi`is	
Hiyyi	tii`as	btii`as	yi`seni	yi`sit	
Hinni	yii`aso	byii`aso	yi`seniin	yi`so	
Niħna	nii`as	mnii`as	yi`seniin	y`isna	

Past Tense Forms

Pronoun + To Be		Past Continuous		Past Habit	Past Perfect	Past Anterior
Ana	kint	xam	ii`as	ii`as	yi`sen	y`ist
Inta	kint	xam	tii`as	tii`as	yi`sen	y`ist
Inti	kinti	xam	tii`asi	tii`asi	yi`seni	y`isti
Into	kinto	xam	tii`aso	tii`aso	yi`seniin	y`isto
Huwwi	ken	xam	yii`as	yii`as	yi`sen	yi`is
Hiyyi	kenit	xam	tii`as	tii`as	yi`seni	yi`sit
Hinni	keno	xam	yii`aso	yii`aso	yi`seniin	yi`so
Niħna	kinna	xam	nii`as	nii`as	yi`seniin	y`isna

Present and Future Tense Forms

Pronoun	Present Continuous		Simple Future		Anterior Future	
Ana	xam	ii`as	raħ	ii`as	kint raħ	ii`as
Inta	xam	tii`as	raħ	tii`as	kint raħ	tii`as
Inti	xam	tii`asi	raħ	tii`asi	kinti raħ	tii`asi
Into	xam	tii`aso	raħ	tii`aso	kinto raħ	tii`aso
Huwwi	xam	yii`as	raħ	yii`as	ken raħ	yii`as
Hiyyi	xam	tii`as	raħ	tii`as	kenit raħ	tii`as
Hinni	xam	yii`aso	raħ	yii`aso	keno raħ	yii`aso
Niħna	xam	nii`as	raħ	nii`as	kinna raħ	nii`as

Notes

This verb group is characterized by the "ii" vowel sound after the infinitive "y". It is a very rare verb group.

Yicte`

To long for | To miss

Group: 6I

Principal Forms

Pronoun	Infinitive	Simple Present	Perfect Present	Simple Past	Imperative
Ana	icte`	bicte`	micte`	cti`t	
Inta	icte`	bicte`	micte`	cti`t	cte`
Inti	ticte`i	bticte`i	micte`a	cti`ti	cte`i
Into	ticte`o	bticte`o	micte`iin	cti`to	cte`o
Huwwi	yicte`	byicte`	micte`	cte`	
Hiyyi	ticte`	bticte`	micte`a	cte`it	
Hinni	yicte`o	byicte`o	micte`iin	cte`o	
Niħna	nicte`	mnicte`	micte`iin	cti`na	

Past Tense Forms

Pronoun + To Be		Past Continuous		Past Habit	Past Perfect	Past Anterior
Ana	kint	xam	icte`	icte`	micte`	cit`t
Inta	kint	xam	icte`	icte`	micte`	cti`t
Inti	kinti	xam	ticte`i	ticte`i	micte`a	cti`ti
Into	kinto	xam	ticte`o	ticte`o	micte`iin	cti`to
Huwwi	ken	xam	yicte`	yicte`	micte`	cte`
Hiyyi	kenit	xam	ticte`	ticte`	micte`a	cte`it
Hinni	keno	xam	yicte`o	yicte`o	micte`iin	cte`o
Niħna	kinna	xam	nicte`	nicte`	micte`iin	cti`na

Present and Future Tense Forms

Pronoun	Present Continuous		Simple Future		Anterior Future	
Ana	xam	icte`	raħ	icte`	kint raħ	icte`
Inta	xam	icte`	raħ	icte`	kint raħ	icte`
Inti	xam	ticte`i	raħ	ticte`i	kinti raħ	ticte`i
Into	xam	ticte`o	raħ	ticte`o	kinto raħ	ticte`o
Huwwi	xam	yicte`	raħ	yicte`	ken raħ	yicte`
Hiyyi	xam	ticte`	raħ	ticte`	kenit raħ	ticte`
Hinni	xam	yicte`o	raħ	yicte`o	keno raħ	yicte`o
Niħna	xam	nicte`	raħ	nicte`	kinna raħ	nicte`

Notes
This verb group is characterized by the vowel "e" before the last consonant in the infinitive form.

Yirsom

To draw

Group: 6Ja

Principal Forms

Pronoun	Infinitive	Simple Present	Perfect Present	Simple Past	Imperative
Ana	irsom	birsom	resim	rasamt	
Inta	tirsom	btirsom	resim	rasamt	rsum
Inti	tirismi	btirismi	resmi	rasamti	rsimi
Into	tirismo	btirismo	resmiin	rasamto	rsimo
Huwwi	yirsom	byirsom	resim	rasam	
Hiyyi	tirsom	btirsom	resmi	rasamit	
Hinni	yirismo	byirismo	resmiin	rasamo	
Niħna	nirsom	mnirsom	resmiin	rasamna	

Past Tense Forms

Pronoun + To Be		Past Continuous		Past Habit	Past Perfect	Past Anterior
Ana	kint	xam	irsom	irsom	resim	rasamt
Inta	kint	xam	tirsom	tirsom	resim	rasamt
Inti	kinti	xam	tirismi	tirismi	resmi	rasamti
Into	kinto	xam	tirismo	tirismo	resmiin	rasamto
Huwwi	ken	xam	yirsom	yirsom	resim	rasam
Hiyyi	kenit	xam	tirsom	tirsom	resmi	rasamit
Hinni	keno	xam	yirismo	yirismo	resmiin	rasamo
Niħna	kinna	xam	nirsom	nirsom	resmiin	rasamna

Present and Future Tense Forms

Pronoun	Present Continuous		Simple Future		Anterior Future	
Ana	xam	irsom	raħ	irsom	kint raħ	irsom
Inta	xam	tirsom	raħ	tirsom	kint raħ	tirsom
Inti	xam	tirismi	raħ	tirismi	kinti raħ	tirismi
Into	xam	tirismo	raħ	tirismo	kinto raħ	tirismo
Huwwi	xam	yirsom	raħ	yirsom	ken raħ	yirsom
Hiyyi	xam	tirsom	raħ	tirsom	kenit raħ	tirsom
Hinni	xam	yirismo	raħ	yirismo	keno raħ	yirismo
Niħna	xam	nirsom	raħ	nirsom	kinna raħ	nirsom

Notes
This is an extremely common verb group. It is advisable to know this group by heart for any student of the Lebanese language.

Yi`lob

To switch | To flip | To tumble

Group: 6Jb

Principal Forms

Pronoun	Infinitive	Simple Present	Perfect Present	Simple Past	Imperative
Ana	i`lob	bi`lob	elib	alabt	
Inta	ti`lob	bti`lob	elib	alabt	`lub
Inti	ti`ilbi	bti`ilbi	elbi	alabti	`libi
Into	ti`ilbo	bti`ilbo	elbiin	alabto	`libo
Huwwi	yi`lob	byi`lob	elib	alab	
Hiyyi	ti`lob	bti`lob	elbi	alabit	
Hinni	yi`ilbo	byi`ilbo	elbiin	alabo	
Niħna	ni`lob	mni`lob	elbiin	alabna	

Past Tense Forms

Pronoun + To Be		Past Continuous		Past Habit	Past Perfect	Past Anterior
Ana	**kint**	xam	i`lob	i`lob	elib	alabt
Inta	**kint**	xam	ti`lob	ti`lob	elib	alabt
Inti	**kinti**	xam	ti`ilbi	ti`ilbi	elbi	alabti
Into	**kinto**	xam	ti`ilbo	ti`ilbo	elbiin	alabto
Huwwi	**ken**	xam	yi`lob	yi`lob	elib	alab
Hiyyi	**kenit**	xam	ti`lob	ti`lob	elbi	alabit
Hinni	**keno**	xam	yi`ilbo	yi`ilbo	elbiin	alabo
Niħna	**kinna**	xam	ni`lob	ni`lob	elbiin	alabna

Present and Future Tense Forms

Pronoun	Present Continuous		Simple Future		Anterior Future	
Ana	xam	i`lob	raħ	i`lob	kint raħ	i`lob
Inta	xam	ti`lob	raħ	ti`lob	kint raħ	ti`lob
Inti	xam	ti`ilbi	raħ	ti`ilbi	kinti raħ	ti`ilbi
Into	xam	ti`ilbo	raħ	ti`ilbo	kinto raħ	ti`ilbo
Huwwi	xam	yi`lob	raħ	yi`lob	ken raħ	yi`lob
Hiyyi	xam	ti`lob	raħ	ti`lob	kenit raħ	ti`lob
Hinni	xam	yi`ilbo	raħ	yi`ilbo	keno raħ	yi`ilbo
Niħna	xam	ni`lob	raħ	ni`lob	kinna raħ	ni`lob

Notes

The aleph sound before a vowel in the verb is not written down in the beginning of the Present Perfect and Simple Past because the vowel expresses the sound ` without a need to write it.

Yiħmol

To carry

Group: 6Jc

Principal Forms

Pronoun	Infinitive	Simple Present	Perfect Present	Simple Past	Imperative
Ana	iħmol	biħmol	ħemil	ħmilt	
Inta	tiħmol	btiħmol	ħemil	ħmilt	ħmul
Inti	tiħimli	btiħimli	ħemli	ħmilti	ħmili
Into	tiħimlo	btiħimlo	ħemliin	ħmilto	ħmilo
Huwwi	yiħmol	byiħmol	ħemil	ħimil	
Hiyyi	tiħmol	btiħmol	ħemli	ħimlit	
Hinni	yiħimlo	byiħimlo	ħemliin	ħimlo	
Niħna	niħmol	mniħmol	ħemliin	ħmilna	

Past Tense Forms

Pronoun + To Be		Past Continuous		Past Habit	Past Perfect	Past Anterior
Ana	kint	xam	iħmol	iħmol	ħemil	ħmilt
Inta	kint	xam	tiħmol	tiħmol	ħemil	ħmilt
Inti	kinti	xam	tiħimli	tiħimli	ħemli	ħmilti
Into	kinto	xam	tiħimlo	tiħimlo	ħemliin	ħmilto
Huwwi	ken	xam	yiħmol	yiħmol	ħemil	ħimil
Hiyyi	kenit	xam	tiħmol	tiħmol	ħemli	ħimlit
Hinni	keno	xam	yiħimlo	yiħimlo	ħemliin	ħimlo
Niħna	kinna	xam	niħmol	niħmol	ħemliin	ħmilna

Present and Future Tense Forms

Pronoun	Present Continuous		Simple Future		Anterior Future	
Ana	xam	iħmol	raħ	iħmol	kint raħ	iħmol
Inta	xam	tiħmol	raħ	tiħmol	kint raħ	tiħmol
Inti	xam	tiħimli	raħ	tiħimli	kinti raħ	tiħimli
Into	xam	tiħimlo	raħ	tiħimlo	kinto raħ	tiħimlo
Huwwi	xam	yiħmol	raħ	yiħmol	ken raħ	yiħmol
Hiyyi	xam	tiħmol	raħ	tiħmol	kenit raħ	tiħmol
Hinni	xam	yiħimlo	raħ	yiħimlo	keno raħ	yiħimlo
Niħna	xam	niħmol	raħ	niħmol	kinna raħ	niħmol

Notes

This subgroup varies from the other subgroups in group 6J by the conjugation of the simple past tense form.

Yictiri

To buy | To purchase

Group: 7A

Principal Forms

Pronoun	Infinitive	Simple Present	Perfect Present	Simple Past	Imperative
Ana	ictiri	bictiri	ceri	ctarayt	
Inta	tictiri	btictiri	ceri	ctarayt	ctrii
Inti	tictiri	btictiri	ceryi	ctarayti	ctrii
Into	tictiro	btictiro	ceryiin	ctarayto	ctru
Huwwi	yictiri	byictiri	ceri	ctara	
Hiyyi	tictiri	btictiri	ceryi	ctarit	
Hinni	yictiro	byictiro	ceryiin	ctaro	
Niħna	nictiri	mnictiri	ceryiin	ctarayna	

Past Tense Forms

Pronoun + To Be		Past Continuous		Past Habit	Past Perfect	Past Anterior
Ana	kint	xam	ictiri	ictiri	ceri	ctarayt
Inta	kint	xam	tictiri	tictiri	ceri	ctarayt
Inti	kinti	xam	tictiri	tictiri	ceryi	ctarayti
Into	kinto	xam	tictiro	tictiro	ceryiin	ctarayto
Huwwi	ken	xam	yictiri	yictiri	ceri	ctara
Hiyyi	kenit	xam	tictiri	tictiri	ceryi	ctarit
Hinni	keno	xam	yictiro	yictiro	ceryiin	ctaro
Niħna	kinna	xam	nictiri	nictiri	ceryiin	ctarayna

Present and Future Tense Forms

Pronoun	Present Continuous		Simple Future		Anterior Future	
Ana	xam	ictiri	raħ	ictiri	kint raħ	ictiri
Inta	xam	tictiri	raħ	tictiri	kint raħ	tictiri
Inti	xam	tictiri	raħ	tictiri	kinti raħ	tictiri
Into	xam	tictiro	raħ	tictiro	kinto raħ	tictiro
Huwwi	xam	yictiri	raħ	yictiri	ken raħ	yictiri
Hiyyi	xam	tictiri	raħ	tictiri	kenit raħ	tictiri
Hinni	xam	yictiro	raħ	yictiro	keno raħ	yictiro
Niħna	xam	nictiri	raħ	nictiri	kinna raħ	nictiri

Notes

This verb group is characterized by the three "i" vowels in the infinitive form.

Yihtamm

Group: 7B

To care | To be concerned about

Principal Forms

Pronoun	Infinitive	Simple Present	Perfect Present	Simple Past	Imperative
Ana	ihtamm	bihtamm	mihtamm	htammayt	
Inta	tihtamm	btihtamm	mihtamm	htammayt	htamm
Inti	tihtammi	btihtammi	mihtammi	htammayti	htammi
Into	tihtammo	btihtammo	mihtammiin	htammayto	htammo
Huwwi	yihtamm	byihtamm	mihtamm	htamm	
Hiyyi	tihtamm	btihtamm	mihtammi	htammit	
Hinni	yihtammo	byihtammo	mihtammiin	htammo	
Niħna	nihtamm	mnihtamm	mihtammiin	htammayna	

Past Tense Forms

Pronoun + To Be		Past Continuous		Past Habit	Past Perfect	Past Anterior
Ana	**kint**	xam	ihtamm	ihtamm	mihtamm	htammayt
Inta	**kint**	xam	tihtamm	tihtamm	mihtamm	htammayt
Inti	**kinti**	xam	tihtammi	tihtammi	mihtammi	htammayti
Into	**kinto**	xam	tihtammo	tihtammo	mihtammiin	htammayto
Huwwi	**ken**	xam	yihtamm	yihtamm	mihtamm	htamm
Hiyyi	**kenit**	xam	tihtamm	tihtamm	mihtammi	htammit
Hinni	**keno**	xam	yihtammo	yihtammo	mihtammiin	htammo
Niħna	**kinna**	xam	nihtamm	nihtamm	mihtammiin	htammayna

Present and Future Tense Forms

Pronoun	Present Continuous		Simple Future		Anterior Future	
Ana	xam	ihtamm	raħ	ihtamm	kint raħ	ihtamm
Inta	xam	tihtamm	raħ	tihtamm	kint raħ	tihtamm
Inti	xam	tihtammi	raħ	tihtammi	kinti raħ	tihtammi
Into	xam	tihtammo	raħ	tihtammo	kinto raħ	tihtammo
Huwwi	xam	yihtamm	raħ	yihtamm	ken raħ	yihtamm
Hiyyi	xam	tihtamm	raħ	tihtamm	kenit raħ	tihtamm
Hinni	xam	yihtammo	raħ	yihtammo	keno raħ	yihtammo
Niħna	xam	nihtamm	raħ	nihtamm	kinna raħ	nihtamm

Notes

This verb group is characterized by the double consonant at the end of the verb.

Yitfeda

To avoid | To dodge

Group: 7C

Principal Forms

Pronoun	Infinitive	Simple Present	Perfect Present	Simple Past	Imperative
Ana	itfeda	bitfeda	mitfedi	tfedayt	
Inta	titfeda	btitfeda	mitfedi	tfedayt	tfeda
Inti	titfedi	btitfedi	mitfedyi	tfedayti	tfedi
Into	titfedo	btitfedo	mitfedyiin	tfedayto	tfedo
Huwwi	yitfeda	byitfeda	mitfedi	tfeda	
Hiyyi	titfeda	btitfeda	mitfedyi	tfedit	
Hinni	yitfedo	byitfedo	mitfedyiin	tfedo	
Niħna	nitfeda	mnitfeda	mitfedyiin	tfedayna	

Past Tense Forms

Pronoun + To Be		Past Continuous		Past Habit	Past Perfect	Past Anterior
Ana	kint	xam	itfeda	itfeda	mitfedi	tfedayt
Inta	kint	xam	titfeda	titfeda	mitfedi	tfedayt
Inti	kinti	xam	titfedi	titfedi	mitfedyi	tfedayti
Into	kinto	xam	titfedo	titfedo	mitfedyiin	tfedayto
Huwwi	ken	xam	yitfeda	yitfeda	mitfedi	tfeda
Hiyyi	kenit	xam	titfeda	titfeda	mitfedyi	tfedit
Hinni	keno	xam	yitfedo	yitfedo	mitfedyiin	tfedo
Niħna	kinna	xam	nitfeda	nitfeda	mitfedyiin	tfedayna

Present and Future Tense Forms

Pronoun	Present Continuous		Simple Future		Anterior Future	
Ana	xam	itfeda	raħ	itfeda	kint raħ	itfeda
Inta	xam	titfeda	raħ	titfeda	kint raħ	titfeda
Inti	xam	titfedi	raħ	titfedi	kinti raħ	titfedi
Into	xam	titfedo	raħ	titfedo	kinto raħ	titfedo
Huwwi	xam	yitfeda	raħ	yitfeda	ken raħ	yitfeda
Hiyyi	xam	titfeda	raħ	titfeda	kenit raħ	titfeda
Hinni	xam	yitfedo	raħ	yitfedo	keno raħ	yitfedo
Niħna	xam	nitfeda	raħ	nitfeda	kinna raħ	nitfeda

Notes
This is not a very common verb group. It is characterized by the vowel "e" before the last consonant in the infinitive.

Yballic

Group: 7Da

To begin | To start

Principal Forms

Pronoun	Infinitive	Simple Present	Perfect Present	Simple Past	Imperative
Ana	ballic	bballic	mballic	ballact	
Inta	tballic	bitballic	mballic	ballact	ballic
Inti	tballci	bitballci	mballci	ballacti	ballci
Into	tballco	bitballco	mballciin	ballacto	ballco
Huwwi	yballic	biballic	mballic	ballac	
Hiyyi	tballic	bitballic	mballci	ballacit	
Hinni	yballco	biballco	mballciin	ballaco	
Niħna	nballic	minballic	mballciin	ballacna	

Past Tense Forms

Pronoun + To Be		Past Continuous		Past Habit	Past Perfect	Past Anterior
Ana	kint	xam	ballic	ballic	mballic	ballact
Inta	kint	xam	tballic	tballic	mballic	ballact
Inti	kinti	xam	tballci	tballci	mballci	ballacti
Into	kinto	xam	tballco	tballco	mballciin	ballacto
Huwwi	ken	xam	yballic	yballic	mballic	ballac
Hiyyi	kenit	xam	tballic	tballic	mballci	ballacit
Hinni	keno	xam	yballico	yballico	mballciin	ballaco
Niħna	kinna	xam	nballic	nballic	mballciin	ballacna

Present and Future Tense Forms

Pronoun	Present Continuous		Simple Future		Anterior Future	
Ana	xam	ballic	raħ	ballic	kint raħ	ballic
Inta	xam	tballic	raħ	tballic	kint raħ	tballic
Inti	xam	tballci	raħ	tballci	kinti raħ	tballci
Into	xam	tballco	raħ	tballco	kinto raħ	tballco
Huwwi	xam	yballic	raħ	yballic	ken raħ	yballic
Hiyyi	xam	tballic	raħ	tballic	kenit raħ	tballic
Hinni	xam	yballico	raħ	yballico	keno raħ	yballico
Niħna	xam	nballic	raħ	nballic	kinna raħ	nballic

Notes

This verb group is extremely common and many essential verbs belong to this group. It is advisable to memorize the rhyming of its conjugation by heart.

Y`affil

To lock

Group: 7Db

Principal Forms

Pronoun	Infinitive	Simple Present	Perfect Present	Simple Past	Imperative
Ana	affil	b`affil	m`affil	affalt	
Inta	t`affil	bit`affil	m`affil	affalt	affil
Inti	t`affli	bit`affli	m`affli	affalti	affli
Into	t`afflo	bit`afflo	m`affliin	affalto	afflo
Huwwi	y`affil	bi`affil	m`affil	affal	
Hiyyi	t`affil	bit`affil	m`affli	affalit	
Hinni	y`afflo	bi`afflo	m`affliin	affalo	
Niħna	n`affil	min`affil	m`affliin	affalna	

Past Tense Forms

Pronoun + To Be		Past Continuous		Past Habit	Past Perfect	Past Anterior
Ana	kint	xam	affil	affil	m`affil	affalt
Inta	kint	xam	t`affil	t`affil	m`affil	affalt
Inti	kinti	xam	t`affli	t`affli	m`affli	affalti
Into	kinto	xam	t`afflo	t`afflo	m`affliin	affalto
Huwwi	ken	xam	y`affil	y`affil	m`affil	affal
Hiyyi	kenit	xam	t`affil	t`affil	m`affli	affalit
Hinni	keno	xam	y`afflo	y`afflo	m`affliin	affalo
Niħna	kinna	xam	n`affil	n`affil	m`affliin	affalna

Present and Future Tense Forms

Pronoun	Present Continuous		Simple Future		Anterior Future	
Ana	xam	affil	raħ	affil	kint raħ	affil
Inta	xam	t`affil	raħ	t`affil	kint raħ	t`affil
Inti	xam	t`affli	raħ	t`affli	kinti raħ	t`affli
Into	xam	t`afflo	raħ	t`afflo	kinto raħ	t`afflo
Huwwi	xam	y`affil	raħ	y`affil	ken raħ	y`affil
Hiyyi	xam	t`affil	raħ	t`affil	kenit raħ	t`affil
Hinni	xam	y`afflo	raħ	y`afflo	keno raħ	y`afflo
Niħna	xam	n`affil	raħ	n`affil	kinna raħ	n`affil

Notes
The aleph sound before a vowel in the verb is not written down in the beginning of the Present Perfect and Simple Past because the vowel expresses the sound ` without a need to write it.

Ybarmij

To program

Group: 7Ea

Principal Forms

Pronoun	Infinitive	Simple Present	Perfect Present	Simple Past	Imperative
Ana	barmij	bbarmij	mbarmij	barmajt	
Inta	tbarmij	bitbarmij	mbarmij	barmajt	barmij
Inti	tbarimji	bitbarimji	mbarimji	barmajti	barimji
Into	tbarimjo	bitbarimjo	mbarimjiin	barmajto	barimjo
Huwwi	ybarmij	bibarmij	mbarmij	barmaj	
Hiyyi	tbarmij	bitbarmij	mbarimji	barmajit	
Hinni	ybarimjo	bibarimjo	mbarimjiin	barmajo	
Niħna	nbarmij	minbarmij	mbarimjiin	barmajna	

Past Tense Forms

Pronoun + To Be		Past Continuous		Past Habit	Past Perfect	Past Anterior
Ana	kint	xam	barmij	barmij	mbarmij	barmajt
Inta	kint	xam	tbarmij	tbarmij	mbarmij	barmajt
Inti	kinti	xam	tbarmji	tbarmji	mbarimji	barmajti
Into	kinto	xam	tbarmjo	tbarmjo	mbarimjiin	barmajto
Huwwi	ken	xam	ybarmij	ybarmij	mbarmij	barmaj
Hiyyi	kenit	xam	tbarmij	tbarmij	mbarimji	barmajit
Hinni	keno	xam	ybarmjo	ybarmjo	mbarimjiin	barmajo
Niħna	kinna	xam	nbarmij	nbarmij	mbarimjiin	barmajna

Present and Future Tense Forms

Pronoun	Present Continuous		Simple Future		Anterior Future	
Ana	xam	barmij	raħ	barmij	kint raħ	barmij
Inta	xam	tbarmij	raħ	tbarmij	kint raħ	tbarmij
Inti	xam	tbarmji	raħ	tbarmji	kinti raħ	tbarmji
Into	xam	tbarmjo	raħ	tbarmjo	kinto raħ	tbarmjo
Huwwi	xam	ybarmij	raħ	ybarmij	ken raħ	ybarmij
Hiyyi	xam	tbarmij	raħ	tbarmij	kenit raħ	tbarmij
Hinni	xam	ybarmjo	raħ	ybarmjo	keno raħ	ybarmjo
Niħna	xam	nbarmij	raħ	nbarmij	kinna raħ	nbarmij

Notes

This group is similar to group 7Da, but it is classified under its group for convenience because the infinitive form does not have a double consonant.

Y`aś`iś

To shred | To cut

Group: 7Eb

Principal Forms

Pronoun	Infinitive	Simple Present	Perfect Present	Simple Past	Imperative
Ana	aś`iś	b`aś`iś	m`aś`iś	aś`aśt	
Inta	t`aś`iś	bit`aś`iś	m`aś`iś	aś`aśt	aś`iś
Inti	t`aśi`śi	bit`aśi`śi	m`aśi`śa	aś`aśti	aśi`śi
Into	t`aśi`śo	bit`aśi`śo	m`aśi`śiin	aś`aśto	aśi`śo
Huwwi	y`aś`iś	bi`aś`iś	m`aś`iś	aś`aś	
Hiyyi	t`aś`iś	bit`aś`iś	m`aśi`śa	aś`aśit	
Hinni	y`aśi`śo	bi`aśi`śo	m`aśi`śiin	aś`aśo	
Niħna	n`aś`iś	min`aś`iś	m`aśi`śiin	aś`aśna	

Past Tense Forms

Pronoun + To Be		Past Continuous		Past Habit	Past Perfect	Past Anterior
Ana	kint	xam	aś`iś	aś`iś	m`aś`iś	aś`aśt
Inta	kint	xam	t`aś`iś	t`aś`iś	m`aś`iś	aś`aśt
Inti	kinti	xam	t`aśi`śi	t`aśi`śi	m`aśi`śa	aś`aśti
Into	kinto	xam	t`aśi`śo	t`aśi`śo	m`aśi`śiin	aś`aśto
Huwwi	ken	xam	y`aś`iś	y`aś`iś	m`aś`iś	aś`aś
Hiyyi	kenit	xam	t`aś`iś	t`aś`iś	m`aśi`śa	aś`aśit
Hinni	keno	xam	y`aśi`śo	y`aśi`śo	m`aśi`śiin	aś`aśo
Niħna	kinna	xam	n`aś`iś	n`aś`iś	m`aśi`śiin	aś`aśna

Present and Future Tense Forms

Pronoun	Present Continuous		Simple Future		Anterior Future	
Ana	xam	aś`iś	raħ	aś`iś	kint raħ	aś`iś
Inta	xam	t`aś`iś	raħ	t`aś`iś	kint raħ	t`aś`iś
Inti	xam	t`aśi`śi	raħ	t`aśi`śi	kinti raħ	t`aśi`śi
Into	xam	t`aśi`śo	raħ	t`aśi`śo	kinto raħ	t`aśi`śo
Huwwi	xam	y`aś`iś	raħ	y`aś`iś	ken raħ	y`aś`iś
Hiyyi	xam	t`aś`iś	raħ	t`aś`iś	kenit raħ	t`aś`iś
Hinni	xam	y`aśi`śo	raħ	y`aśi`śo	keno raħ	y`aśi`śo
Niħna	xam	n`aś`iś	raħ	n`aś`iś	kinna raħ	n`aś`iś

Notes

The aleph sound before a vowel in the verb is not written down in the beginning of the Present Perfect and Simple Past because the vowel expresses the sound ` without a need to write it.

Yḋaayin

To last

Group: 7Fa

Principal Forms

Pronoun	Infinitive	Simple Present	Perfect Present	Simple Past	Imperative
Ana	ḋaayin	bḋaayin	mḋaayin	ḋaayant	
Inta	tḋaayin	bitḋaayin	mḋaayin	ḋaayant	ḋaayin
Inti	tḋaayni	bitḋaayni	mḋaayni	ḋaayanti	ḋaayni
Into	tḋaayno	bitḋaayno	mḋaayniin	ḋaayanto	ḋaayno
Huwwi	yḋaayin	biḋaayin	mḋaayin	ḋaayan	
Hiyyi	tḋaayin	bitḋaayin	mḋaayni	ḋaayanit	
Hinni	yḋaayno	biḋaayno	mḋaayniin	ḋaayano	
Niħna	nḋaayin	minḋaayin	mḋaayniin	ḋaayanna	

Past Tense Forms

Pronoun + To Be		Past Continuous		Past Habit	Past Perfect	Past Anterior
Ana	kint	xam	ḋaayin	ḋaayin	mḋaayin	ḋaayant
Inta	kint	xam	tḋaayin	tḋaayin	mḋaayin	ḋaayant
Inti	kinti	xam	tḋaayni	tḋaayni	mḋaayni	ḋaayanti
Into	kinto	xam	tḋaayno	tḋaayno	mḋaayniin	ḋaayanto
Huwwi	ken	xam	yḋaayin	yḋaayin	mḋaayin	ḋaayan
Hiyyi	kenit	xam	tḋaayin	tḋaayin	mḋaayni	ḋaayanit
Hinni	keno	xam	yḋaayno	yḋaayno	mḋaayniin	ḋaayano
Niħna	kinna	xam	nḋaayin	nḋaayin	mḋaayniin	ḋaayanna

Present and Future Tense Forms

Pronoun	Present Continuous		Simple Future		Anterior Future	
Ana	xam	ḋaayin	raħ	ḋaayin	kint raħ	ḋaayin
Inta	xam	tḋaayin	raħ	tḋaayin	kint raħ	tḋaayin
Inti	xam	tḋaayni	raħ	tḋaayni	kinti raħ	tḋaayni
Into	xam	tḋaayno	raħ	tḋaayno	kinto raħ	tḋaayno
Huwwi	xam	yḋaayin	raħ	yḋaayin	ken raħ	yḋaayin
Hiyyi	xam	tḋaayin	raħ	tḋaayin	kenit raħ	tḋaayin
Hinni	xam	yḋaayno	raħ	yḋaayno	keno raħ	yḋaayno
Niħna	xam	nḋaayin	raħ	nḋaayin	kinna raħ	nḋaayin

Notes

This group is identified by the double "aa" vowel.

Y`aarin

To compare

Group: 7Fb

Principal Forms

Pronoun	Infinitive	Simple Present	Perfect Present	Simple Past	Imperative
Ana	aarin	b`aarin	m`aarin	aarant	
Inta	t`aarin	bit`aarin	m`aarin	aarant	aarin
Inti	t`aarni	bit`aarni	m`aarna	aaranti	aarni
Into	t`aarno	bit`aarno	m`aarniin	aaranto	aarno
Huwwi	y`aarin	bi`aarin	m`aarin	aaran	
Hiyyi	t`aarin	bit`aarin	m`aarna	aaranit	
Hinni	y`aarno	bi`aarno	m`aarniin	aarano	
Niħna	n`aarin	min`aarin	m`aarniin	aaranna	

Past Tense Forms

Pronoun + To Be		Past Continuous		Past Habit	Past Perfect	Past Anterior
Ana	kint	xam	aarin	aarin	m`aarin	aarant
Inta	kint	xam	t`aarin	t`aarin	m`aarin	aarant
Inti	kinti	xam	t`aarni	t`aarni	m`aarna	aaranti
Into	kinto	xam	t`aarno	t`aarno	m`aarniin	aaranto
Huwwi	ken	xam	y`aarin	y`aarin	m`aarin	aaran
Hiyyi	kenit	xam	t`aarin	t`aarin	m`aarna	aaranit
Hinni	keno	xam	y`aarno	y`aarno	m`aarniin	aarano
Niħna	kinna	xam	n`aarin	n`aarin	m`aarniin	aaranna

Present and Future Tense Forms

Pronoun	Present Continuous		Simple Future		Anterior Future	
Ana	xam	aarin	raħ	aarin	kint raħ	aarin
Inta	xam	t`aarin	raħ	t`aarin	kint raħ	t`aarin
Inti	xam	t`aarni	raħ	t`aarni	kinti raħ	t`aarni
Into	xam	t`aarno	raħ	t`aarno	kinto raħ	t`aarno
Huwwi	xam	y`aarin	raħ	y`aarin	ken raħ	y`aarin
Hiyyi	xam	t`aarin	raħ	t`aarin	kenit raħ	t`aarin
Hinni	xam	y`aarno	raħ	y`aarno	keno raħ	y`aarno
Niħna	xam	n`aarin	raħ	n`aarin	kinna raħ	n`aarin

Notes
The aleph sound before a vowel in the verb is not written down in the beginning of the Present Perfect and Simple Past because the vowel expresses the sound ` without a need to write it.

Yibtisim

To smile

Group: 8Aa

Principal Forms

Pronoun	Infinitive	Simple Present	Perfect Present	Simple Past	Imperative
Ana	ibtisim	bibtisim	mibtisim	btasamt	
Inta	tibtisim	btibtisim	mibtisim	btasamt	btisim
Inti	tibtismi	btibtismi	mibtismi	btasamti	btismi
Into	tibtismo	btibtismo	mibtismiin	btasamto	btismo
Huwwi	yibtisim	byibtisim	mibtisim	btasam	
Hiyyi	tibtisim	btibtisim	mibtismi	btasamit	
Hinni	yibtismo	byibtismo	mibtismiin	btasamo	
Niħna	nibtisim	mnibtisim	mibtismiin	btasamna	

Past Tense Forms

Pronoun + To Be		Past Continuous		Past Habit	Past Perfect	Past Anterior
Ana	kint	xam	ibtisim	ibtisim	mibtisim	btasamt
Inta	kint	xam	tibtisim	tibtisim	mibtisim	btasamt
Inti	kinti	xam	tibtismi	tibtismi	mibtismi	btasamti
Into	kinto	xam	tibtismo	tibtismo	mibtismiin	btasamto
Huwwi	ken	xam	yibtisim	yibtisim	mibtisim	btasam
Hiyyi	kenit	xam	tibtisim	tibtisim	mibtismi	btasamit
Hinni	keno	xam	yibtismo	yibtismo	mibtismiin	btasamo
Niħna	kinna	xam	nibtisim	nibtisim	mibtismiin	btasamna

Present and Future Tense Forms

Pronoun	Present Continuous		Simple Future		Anterior Future	
Ana	xam	ibtisim	raħ	ibtisim	kint raħ	ibtisim
Inta	xam	tibtisim	raħ	tibtisim	kint raħ	tibtisim
Inti	xam	tibtismi	raħ	tibtismi	kinti raħ	tibtismi
Into	xam	tibtismo	raħ	tibtismo	kinto raħ	tibtismo
Huwwi	xam	yibtisim	raħ	yibtisim	ken raħ	yibtisim
Hiyyi	xam	tibtisim	raħ	tibtisim	kenit raħ	tibtisim
Hinni	xam	yibtismo	raħ	yibtismo	keno raħ	yibtismo
Niħna	xam	nibtisim	raħ	nibtisim	kinna raħ	nibtisim

Notes
This verb group is characterized by the three “i” vowels.

Yonboṡiṫ

To be happy

Group: 8Ab

Principal Forms

Pronoun	Infinitive	Simple Present	Perfect Present	Simple Past	Imperative
Ana	onboṡiṫ	bonboṡiṫ	monboṡiṫ	nbaṡaṫṫ	
Inta	tonboṡiṫ	btonboṡiṫ	monboṡiṫ	nbaṡaṫṫ	nboṡiṫ
Inti	tonboṡṫi	btonboṡṫi	monboṡṫi	nbaṡaṫṫi	nboṡṫi
Into	tonboṡṫo	btonboṡṫo	monboṡṫiin	nbaṡaṫṫo	nboṡṫo
Huwwi	yonboṡiṫ	byonboṡiṫ	monboṡiṫ	nbaṡaṫ	
Hiyyi	tonboṡiṫ	btonboṡiṫ	monboṡṫi	nbaṡaṫit	
Hinni	yonboṡṫo	byonboṡṫo	monboṡṫiin	nbaṡaṫo	
Niħna	nonboṡiṫ	mnonboṡiṫ	monboṡṫiin	nbaṡaṫna	

Past Tense Forms

Pronoun + To Be		Past Continuous		Past Habit	Past Perfect	Past Anterior
Ana	kint	xam	onboṡiṫ	onboṡiṫ	monboṡiṫ	nbaṡaṫṫ
Inta	kint	xam	tonboṡiṫ	tonboṡiṫ	monboṡiṫ	nbaṡaṫṫ
Inti	kinti	xam	tonboṡṫi	tonboṡṫi	monboṡṫi	nbaṡaṫṫi
Into	kinto	xam	tonboṡṫo	tonboṡṫo	monboṡṫiin	nbaṡaṫṫo
Huwwi	ken	xam	yonboṡiṫ	yonboṡiṫ	monboṡiṫ	nbaṡaṫ
Hiyyi	kenit	xam	tonboṡiṫ	tonboṡiṫ	monboṡṫi	nbaṡaṫit
Hinni	keno	xam	yonboṡṫo	yonboṡṫo	monboṡṫiin	nbaṡaṫo
Niħna	kinna	xam	nonboṡiṫ	nonboṡiṫ	monboṡṫiin	nbaṡaṫna

Present and Future Tense Forms

Pronoun	Present Continuous		Simple Future		Anterior Future	
Ana	xam	onboṡiṫ	raħ	onboṡiṫ	kint raħ	onboṡiṫ
Inta	xam	tonboṡiṫ	raħ	tonboṡiṫ	kint raħ	tonboṡiṫ
Inti	xam	tonboṡṫi	raħ	tonboṡṫi	kinti raħ	tonboṡṫi
Into	xam	tonboṡṫo	raħ	tonboṡṫo	kinto raħ	tonboṡṫo
Huwwi	xam	yonboṡiṫ	raħ	yonboṡiṫ	ken raħ	yonboṡiṫ
Hiyyi	xam	tonboṡiṫ	raħ	tonboṡiṫ	kenit raħ	tonboṡiṫ
Hinni	xam	yonboṡṫo	raħ	yonboṡṫo	keno raħ	yonboṡṫo
Niħna	xam	nonboṡiṫ	raħ	nonboṡiṫ	kinna raħ	nonboṡiṫ

Notes
Some Lebanese accents substitute the "o" vowel for an "i" in the second letter of this verb. This does not change the rules of conjugation though.

Yistarji

To dare

Group: 8B

Principal Forms

Pronoun	Infinitive	Simple Present	Perfect Present	Simple Past	Imperative
Ana	istarji	bistarji	mistarji	starjayt	
Inta	tistarji	btistarji	mistarji	starjayt	starji
Inti	tistarji	btistarji	mistarjiyyi	starjayti	starji
Into	tistarjo	btistarjo	mistarjyiin	starjayto	starjo
Huwwi	yistarji	byistarji	mistarji	starja	
Hiyyi	tistarji	btistarji	mistarjiyyi	starjit	
Hinni	yistarjo	byistarjo	mistarjyiin	starjo	
Niħna	nistarji	mnistarji	mistarjyiin	starjayna	

Past Tense Forms

Pronoun + To Be		Past Continuous		Past Habit	Past Perfect	Past Anterior
Ana	**kint**	xam	istarji	istarji	mistarji	starjayt
Inta	**kint**	xam	tistarji	tistarji	mistarji	starjayt
Inti	**kinti**	xam	tistarji	tistarji	mistarjiyyi	starjayti
Into	**kinto**	xam	tistarjo	tistarjo	mistarjyiin	starjayto
Huwwi	**ken**	xam	yistarji	yistarji	mistarji	starja
Hiyyi	**kenit**	xam	tistarji	tistarji	mistarjiyyi	starjit
Hinni	**keno**	xam	yistarjo	yistarjo	mistarjyiin	starjo
Niħna	**kinna**	xam	nistarji	nistarji	mistarjyiin	starjayna

Present and Future Tense Forms

Pronoun	Present Continuous		Simple Future		Anterior Future	
Ana	xam	istarji	raħ	istarji	kint raħ	istarji
Inta	xam	tistarji	raħ	tistarji	kint raħ	tistarji
Inti	xam	tistarji	raħ	tistarji	kinti raħ	tistarji
Into	xam	tistarjo	raħ	tistarjo	kinto raħ	tistarjo
Huwwi	xam	yistarji	raħ	yistarji	ken raħ	yistarji
Hiyyi	xam	tistarji	raħ	tistarji	kenit raħ	tistarji
Hinni	xam	yistarjo	raħ	yistarjo	keno raħ	yistarjo
Niħna	xam	nistarji	raħ	nistarji	kinna raħ	nistarji

Notes

This is not a very common verb group in the Lebanese language.

yitKabba

Yithajja

To spell

Group: 8C

Principal Forms

Pronoun	Infinitive	Simple Present	Perfect Present	Simple Past	Imperative
Ana	ithajja	bithajja	mithajji	thajjayt	
Inta	tithajja	btithajja	mithajji	thajjayt	thajja
Inti	tithajji	btithajji	mithajjeyyi	thajjayti	thajja
Into	tithajjo	btithajjo	mithajjyiin	thajjayto	thajji
Huwwi	yithajja	byithajja	mithajji	thajja	
Hiyyi	tithajja	btithajja	mithajjeyyi	thajjit	
Hinni	yithajjo	byithajjo	mithajjyiin	thajjo	
Niħna	nithajja	mnithajja	mithajjyiin	thajjayna	

Past Tense Forms

Pronoun + To Be		Past Continuous		Past Habit	Past Perfect	Past Anterior
Ana	kint	xam	ithajja	ithajja	mithajji	thajjayt
Inta	kint	xam	tithajja	tithajja	mithajji	thajjayt
Inti	kinti	xam	tithajji	tithajji	mithajjeyyi	thajjayti
Into	kinto	xam	tithajjo	tithajjo	mithajjyiin	thajjayto
Huwwi	ken	xam	yithajja	yithajja	mithajji	thajja
Hiyyi	kenit	xam	tithajja	tithajja	mithajjeyyi	thajjit
Hinni	keno	xam	yithajjo	yithajjo	mithajjyiin	thajjo
Niħna	kinna	xam	nithajja	nithajja	mithajjyiin	thajjayna

Present and Future Tense Forms

Pronoun	Present Continuous		Simple Future		Anterior Future	
Ana	xam	ithajja	raħ	ithajja	kint raħ	ithajja
Inta	xam	tithajja	raħ	tithajja	kint raħ	tithajja
Inti	xam	tithajji	raħ	tithajji	kinti raħ	tithajji
Into	xam	tithajjo	raħ	tithajjo	kinto raħ	tithajjo
Huwwi	xam	yithajja	raħ	yithajja	ken raħ	yithajja
Hiyyi	xam	tithajja	raħ	tithajja	kenit raħ	tithajja
Hinni	xam	yithajjo	raħ	yithajjo	keno raħ	yithajjo
Niħna	xam	nithajja	raħ	nithajja	kinna raħ	nithajja

Notes

This verb group is characterized by the double consonant before the last vowel in the infinitive.

Yitketar

To multiply

Group: 8Da

Principal Forms

Pronoun	Infinitive	Simple Present	Perfect Present	Simple Past	Imperative
Ana	itketar	bitketar	mitketar	tketart	
Inta	titketar	btitketar	mitketar	tketart	tketar
Inti	titketari	btitketari	mitketra	tketarti	tketari
Into	titketaro	btitketaro	mitketriin	tketarto	tketaro
Huwwi	yitketar	byitketar	mitketar	tketar	
Hiyyi	titketar	btitketar	mitketra	tketarit	
Hinni	yitketaro	byitketaro	mitketriin	tketaro	
Niħna	nitketar	mnitketar	mitketriin	tketarna	

Past Tense Forms

Pronoun + To Be		Past Continuous		Past Habit	Past Perfect	Past Anterior
Ana	kint	xam	itketar	itketar	mitketar	tketart
Inta	kint	xam	titketar	titketar	mitketar	tketart
Inti	kinti	xam	titketari	titketari	mitketra	tketarti
Into	kinto	xam	titketaro	titketaro	mitketriin	tketarto
Huwwi	ken	xam	yitketar	yitketar	mitketar	tketar
Hiyyi	kenit	xam	titketar	titketar	mitketra	tketarit
Hinni	keno	xam	yitketaro	yitketaro	mitketriin	tketaro
Niħna	kinna	xam	nitketar	nitketar	mitketriin	tketarna

Present and Future Tense Forms

Pronoun	Present Continuous		Simple Future		Anterior Future	
Ana	xam	itketar	raħ	itketar	kint raħ	itketar
Inta	xam	titketar	raħ	titketar	kint raħ	titketar
Inti	xam	titketari	raħ	titketari	kinti raħ	titketari
Into	xam	titketaro	raħ	titketaro	kinto raħ	titketaro
Huwwi	xam	yitketar	raħ	yitketar	ken raħ	yitketar
Hiyyi	xam	titketar	raħ	titketar	kenit raħ	titketar
Hinni	xam	yitketaro	raħ	yitketaro	keno raħ	yitketaro
Niħna	xam	nitketar	raħ	nitketar	kinna raħ	nitketar

Notes
This is a fairly common verb group in the Lebanese language.

Yistehil

To deserve

Group: 8Db

Principal Forms

Pronoun	Infinitive	Simple Present	Perfect Present	Simple Past	Imperative
Ana	istehil	bistehil	mistehil	stehalt	
Inta	tistehil	btistehil	mistehil	stehalt	stehil
Inti	tistehli	btistehli	mistehli	stehalti	stehli
Into	tistehlo	btistehlo	mistehliin	stehalto	stehlo
Huwwi	yistehil	byistehil	mistehil	stehal	
Hiyyi	tistehil	btistehil	mistehli	stehalit	
Hinni	yistehlo	byistehlo	mistehliin	stehalo	
Niħna	nistehil	mnistehil	mistehliin	stehalna	

Past Tense Forms

Pronoun + To Be		Past Continuous		Past Habit	Past Perfect	Past Anterior
Ana	kint	xam	istehil	istehil	mistehil	stehalt
Inta	kint	xam	tistehil	tistehil	mistehil	stehalt
Inti	kinti	xam	tistehli	tistehli	mistehli	stehalti
Into	kinto	xam	tistehlo	tistehlo	mistehliin	stehalto
Huwwi	ken	xam	yistehil	yistehil	mistehil	stehal
Hiyyi	kenit	xam	tistehil	tistehil	mistehli	stehalit
Hinni	keno	xam	yistehlo	yistehlo	mistehliin	stehalo
Niħna	kinna	xam	nistehil	nistehil	mistehliin	stehalna

Present and Future Tense Forms

Pronoun	Present Continuous		Simple Future		Anterior Future	
Ana	xam	istehil	raħ	istehil	kint raħ	istehil
Inta	xam	tistehil	raħ	tistehil	kint raħ	tistehil
Inti	xam	tistehli	raħ	tistehli	kinti raħ	tistehli
Into	xam	tistehlo	raħ	tistehlo	kinto raħ	tistehlo
Huwwi	xam	yistehil	raħ	yistehil	ken raħ	yistehil
Hiyyi	xam	tistehil	raħ	tistehil	kenit raħ	tistehil
Hinni	xam	yistehlo	raħ	yistehlo	keno raħ	yistehlo
Niħna	xam	nistehil	raħ	nistehil	kinna raħ	nistehil

Notes

This verb group is very rare. It is is similar to the previous group with the exception that it has the vowel "i" before last instead of "a".

Yistxiir

To borrow

Group: 8E

Principal Forms

Pronoun	Infinitive	Simple Present	Perfect Present	Simple Past	Imperative
Ana	istxiir	bistxiir	mistxiir	staxart	
Inta	tistxiir	btistxiir	mistxiir	staxart	stxiir
Inti	tistxiiri	btistxiiri	mistxiiri	staxarti	stxiiri
Into	tistxiiro	btistxiiro	mistxiiriin	staxarto	stxiiro
Huwwi	yistxiir	byistxiir	mistxiir	staxer	
Hiyyi	tistxiir	btistxiir	mistxiiri	staxerit	
Hinni	yistxiiro	byistxiiro	mistxiiriin	staxero	
Niħna	nistxiir	mnistxiir	mistxiiriin	staxarna	

Past Tense Forms

Pronoun + To Be		Past Continuous		Past Habit	Past Perfect	Past Anterior
Ana	kint	xam	istxiir	istxiir	mistxiir	staxart
Inta	kint	xam	tistxiir	tistxiir	mistxiir	staxart
Inti	kinti	xam	tistxiiri	tistxiiri	mistxiiri	staxarti
Into	kinto	xam	tistxiiro	tistxiiro	mistxiiriin	staxarto
Huwwi	ken	xam	yistxiir	yistxiir	mistxiir	staxer
Hiyyi	kenit	xam	tistxiir	tistxiir	mistxiiri	staxerit
Hinni	keno	xam	yistxiiro	yistxiiro	mistxiiriin	staxero
Niħna	kinna	xam	nistxiir	nistxiir	mistxiiriin	staxarna

Present and Future Tense Forms

Pronoun	Present Continuous		Simple Future		Anterior Future	
Ana	xam	istxiir	raħ	istxiir	kint raħ	istxiir
Inta	xam	tistxiir	raħ	tistxiir	kint raħ	tistxiir
Inti	xam	tistxiiri	raħ	tistxiiri	kinti raħ	tistxiiri
Into	xam	tistxiiro	raħ	tistxiiro	kinto raħ	tistxiiro
Huwwi	xam	yistxiir	raħ	yistxiir	ken raħ	yistxiir
Hiyyi	xam	tistxiir	raħ	tistxiir	kenit raħ	tistxiir
Hinni	xam	yistxiiro	raħ	yistxiiro	keno raħ	yistxiiro
Niħna	xam	nistxiir	raħ	nistxiir	kinna raħ	nistxiir

Notes

This is a very rare group. In this book, this is the only verb that belongs to such group.

Yistaxmil

To use

Group: 9A

Principal Forms

Pronoun	Infinitive	Simple Present	Perfect Present	Simple Past	Imperative
Ana	istaxmil	bistaxmil	mistaxmil	staxmalt	
Inta	tistaxmil	btistaxmil	mistaxmil	staxmalt	staxmil
Inti	tistaximli	btistaximli	mistaximli	staxmalti	staximli
Into	tistaximlo	btistaximlo	mistaximliin	staxmalto	staximlo
Huwwi	yistaxmil	byistaxmil	mistaxmil	staxmal	
Hiyyi	tistaxmil	btistaxmil	mistaximli	staxmalit	
Hinni	yistaximlo	byistaximlo	mistaximliin	staxmalo	
Niħna	nistaxmil	mnistaxmil	mistaximliin	staxmalna	

Past Tense Forms

Pronoun + To Be		Past Continuous		Past Habit	Past Perfect	Past Anterior
Ana	kint	xam	istaxmil	istaxmil	mistaxmil	staxmalt
Inta	kint	xam	tistaxmil	tistaxmil	mistaxmil	staxmalt
Inti	kinti	xam	tistaximli	tistaximli	mistaximli	staxmalti
Into	kinto	xam	tistaximlo	tistaximlo	mistaximliin	staxmalto
Huwwi	ken	xam	yistaxmil	yistaxmil	mistaxmil	staxmal
Hiyyi	kenit	xam	tistaxmil	tistaxmil	mistaximli	staxmalit
Hinni	keno	xam	yistaximlo	yistaximlo	mistaximliin	staxmalo
Niħna	kinna	xam	nistaxmil	nistaxmil	mistaximliin	staxmalna

Present and Future Tense Forms

Pronoun	Present Continuous		Simple Future		Anterior Future	
Ana	xam	istaxmil	raħ	istaxmil	kint raħ	istaxmil
Inta	xam	tistaxmil	raħ	tistaxmil	kint raħ	tistaxmil
Inti	xam	tistaximli	raħ	tistaximli	kinti raħ	tistaximli
Into	xam	tistaximlo	raħ	tistaximlo	kinto raħ	tistaximlo
Huwwi	xam	yistaxmil	raħ	yistaxmil	ken raħ	yistaxmil
Hiyyi	xam	tistaxmil	raħ	tistaxmil	kenit raħ	tistaxmil
Hinni	xam	yistaximlo	raħ	yistaximlo	keno raħ	yistaximlo
Niħna	xam	nistaxmil	raħ	nistaxmil	kinna raħ	nistaxmil

Notes

Verbs that contain eigh and nine letters in the infinitive form are easy to conjugate because they follow a very closely related pattern.

Yistafiid

To benefit

Group: 9B

Principal Forms

Pronoun	Infinitive	Simple Present	Perfect Present	Simple Past	Imperative
Ana	istafiid	bistafiid	mistafiid	stafadt	
Inta	tistafiid	btistafiid	mistafiid	stafadt	stafiid
Inti	tistafiidi	btistafiidi	mistafiidi	stafadti	stafiidi
Into	tistafiido	btistafiido	mistafiidiin	stafadto	stafiido
Huwwi	yistafiid	byistafiid	mistafiid	stafed	
Hiyyi	tistafiid	btistafiid	mistafiidi	stafedit	
Hinni	yistafiido	byistafiido	mistafiidiin	stafedo	
Niħna	nistafiid	mnistafiid	mistafiidiin	stafadna	

Past Tense Forms

Pronoun + To Be		Past Continuous		Past Habit	Past Perfect	Past Anterior
Ana	kint	xam	istafiid	istafiid	mistafiid	stafadt
Inta	kint	xam	tistafiid	tistafiid	mistafiid	stafadt
Inti	kinti	xam	tistafiidi	tistafiidi	mistafiidi	stafadti
Into	kinto	xam	tistafiido	tistafiido	mistafiidiin	stafadto
Huwwi	ken	xam	yistafiid	yistafiid	mistafiid	stafed
Hiyyi	kenit	xam	tistafiid	tistafiid	mistafiidi	stafedit
Hinni	keno	xam	yistafiido	yistafiido	mistafiidiin	stafedo
Niħna	kinna	xam	nistafiid	nistafiid	mistafiidiin	stafadna

Present and Future Tense Forms

Pronoun	Present Continuous		Simple Future		Anterior Future	
Ana	xam	istafiid	raħ	istafiid	kint raħ	istafiid
Inta	xam	tistafiid	raħ	tistafiid	kint raħ	tistafiid
Inti	xam	tistafiidi	raħ	tistafiidi	kinti raħ	tistafiidi
Into	xam	tistafiido	raħ	tistafiido	kinto raħ	tistafiido
Huwwi	xam	yistafiid	raħ	yistafiid	ken raħ	yistafiid
Hiyyi	xam	tistafiid	raħ	tistafiid	kenit raħ	tistafiid
Hinni	xam	yistafiido	raħ	yistafiido	keno raħ	yistafiido
Niħna	xam	nistafiid	raħ	nistafiid	kinna raħ	nistafiid

Notes

This verb group is characterized by the "ii" vowel sound before the last letter.

Yistaxidd

To be ready

Group: 9C

Principal Forms

Pronoun	Infinitive	Simple Present	Perfect Present	Simple Past	Imperative
Ana	istaxidd	bistaxidd	mistaxidd	staxaddayt	
Inta	tistaxidd	btistaxidd	mistaxidd	staxaddayt	staxidd
Inti	tistaxiddi	btistaxiddi	mistaxiddi	staxaddayti	staxiddi
Into	tistaxiddo	btistaxiddo	mistaxiddiin	staxaddayto	staxiddo
Huwwi	yistaxidd	byistaxidd	mistaxidd	staxadd	
Hiyyi	tistaxidd	btistaxidd	mistaxiddi	staxaddit	
Hinni	yistaxiddo	byistaxiddo	mistaxiddiin	staxaddo	
Niħna	nistaxidd	mnistaxidd	mistaxiddiin	staxaddayna	

Past Tense Forms

Pronoun + To Be		Past Continuous		Past Habit	Past Perfect	Past Anterior
Ana	kint	xam	istaxidd	istaxidd	mistaxidd	staxaddayt
Inta	kint	xam	tistaxidd	tistaxidd	mistaxidd	staxaddayt
Inti	kinti	xam	tistaxiddi	tistaxiddi	mistaxiddi	staxaddayti
Into	kinto	xam	tistaxiddo	tistaxiddo	mistaxiddiin	staxaddayto
Huwwi	ken	xam	yistaxidd	yistaxidd	mistaxidd	staxadd
Hiyyi	kenit	xam	tistaxidd	tistaxidd	mistaxiddi	staxaddit
Hinni	keno	xam	yistaxiddo	yistaxiddo	mistaxiddiin	staxaddo
Niħna	kinna	xam	nistaxidd	nistaxidd	mistaxiddiin	staxaddayna

Present and Future Tense Forms

Pronoun	Present Continuous		Simple Future		Anterior Future	
Ana	xam	istaxidd	raħ	istaxidd	kint raħ	istaxidd
Inta	xam	tistaxidd	raħ	tistaxidd	kint raħ	tistaxidd
Inti	xam	tistaxiddi	raħ	tistaxiddi	kinti raħ	tistaxiddi
Into	xam	tistaxiddo	raħ	tistaxiddo	kinto raħ	tistaxiddo
Huwwi	xam	yistaxidd	raħ	yistaxidd	ken raħ	yistaxidd
Hiyyi	xam	tistaxidd	raħ	tistaxidd	kenit raħ	tistaxidd
Hinni	xam	yistaxiddo	raħ	yistaxiddo	keno raħ	yistaxiddo
Niħna	xam	nistaxidd	raħ	nistaxidd	kinna raħ	nistaxidd

Notes
This verb group is characterized by the double consonant at the end of the word.

Yistwa``a

To be careful

Group: 9D

Principal Forms

Pronoun	Infinitive	Simple Present	Perfect Present	Simple Past	Imperative
Ana	istwa``a	bistwa``a	mistwa``i	stwa``ayt	
Inta	tistwa``a	btistwa``a	mistwa``i	stwa``ayt	stwa``a
Inti	tistwa``i	btistwa``i	mistwa``yi	stwa``ayti	stwa``i
Into	tistwa``o	btistwa``o	mistwa``yiin	stwa``ayto	stwa``o
Huwwi	yistwa``a	byistwa``a	mistwa``i	stwa``a	
Hiyyi	tistwa``a	btistwa``a	mistwa``yi	stwa``it	
Hinni	yistwa``o	byistwa``o	mistwa``yiin	stwa``o	
Niĥna	nistwa``a	mnistwa``a	mistwa``yiin	stwa``ayna	

Past Tense Forms

Pronoun + To Be		Past Continuous		Past Habit	Past Perfect	Past Anterior
Ana	kint	xam	istwa``a	istwa``a	mistwa``i	stwa``ayt
Inta	kint	xam	tistwa``a	tistwa``a	mistwa``i	stwa``ayt
Inti	kinti	xam	tistwa``i	tistwa``i	mistwa``yi	stwa``ayti
Into	kinto	xam	tistwa``o	tistwa``o	mistwa``yiin	stwa``ayto
Huwwi	ken	xam	yistwa``a	yistwa``a	mistwa``i	stwa``a
Hiyyi	kenit	xam	tistwa``a	tistwa``a	mistwa``yi	stwa``it
Hinni	keno	xam	yistwa``o	yistwa``o	mistwa``yiin	stwa``o
Niĥna	kinna	xam	nistwa``a	nistwa``a	mistwa``yiin	stwa``ayna

Present and Future Tense Forms

Pronoun	Present Continuous		Simple Future		Anterior Future	
Ana	xam	istwa``a	raĥ	istwa``a	kint raĥ	istwa``a
Inta	xam	tistwa``a	raĥ	tistwa``a	kint raĥ	tistwa``a
Inti	xam	tistwa``i	raĥ	tistwa``i	kinti raĥ	tistwa``i
Into	xam	tistwa``o	raĥ	tistwa``o	kinto raĥ	tistwa``o
Huwwi	xam	yistwa``a	raĥ	yistwa``a	ken raĥ	yistwa``a
Hiyyi	xam	tistwa``a	raĥ	tistwa``a	kenit raĥ	tistwa``a
Hinni	xam	yistwa``o	raĥ	yistwa``o	keno raĥ	yistwa``o
Niĥna	xam	nistwa``a	raĥ	nistwa``a	kinna raĥ	nistwa``a

Notes
This verb group is characterized by the double consonant before the last vowel at the end of the word.

Yitsammax

To listen

Group: 9E

Principal Forms

Pronoun	Infinitive	Simple Present	Perfect Present	Simple Past	Imperative
Ana	itsammax	bitsammax	mitsammax	tsammaxt	
Inta	titsammax	btitsammax	mitsammax	tsammaxt	tsammax
Inti	titsammaxi	btitsammaxi	mitsammxa	tsammaxti	tsammaxi
Into	titsammaxo	btitsammaxo	mitsammxiin	tsammaxto	tsammaxo
Huwwi	yitsammax	byitsammax	mitsammax	tsammax	
Hiyyi	titsammax	btitsammax	mitsammxa	tsammaxit	
Hinni	yitsammaxo	byitsammaxo	mitsammxiin	tsammaxo	
Niħna	nitsammax	mnitsammax	mitsammxiin	tsammaxna	

Past Tense Forms

Pronoun + To Be		Past Continuous		Past Habit	Past Perfect	Past Anterior
Ana	kint	xam	itsammax	itsammax	mitsammax	tsammaxayt
Inta	kint	xam	titsammax	titsammax	mitsammax	tsammaxayt
Inti	kinti	xam	titsammaxi	titsammaxi	mitsammxa	tsammaxayti
Into	kinto	xam	titsammaxo	titsammaxo	mitsammxiin	tsammaxayto
Huwwi	ken	xam	yitsammax	yitsammax	mitsammax	tsammax
Hiyyi	kenit	xam	titsammax	titsammax	mitsammxa	tsammaxit
Hinni	keno	xam	yitsammaxo	yitsammaxo	mitsammxiin	tsammaxo
Niħna	kinna	xam	nitsammax	nitsammax	mitsammxiin	tsammaxayna

Present and Future Tense Forms

Pronoun	Present Continuous		Simple Future		Anterior Future	
Ana	xam	itsammax	raħ	itsammax	kint raħ	itsammax
Inta	xam	titsammax	raħ	titsammax	kint raħ	titsammax
Inti	xam	titsammaxi	raħ	titsammaxi	kinti raħ	titsammaxi
Into	xam	titsammaxo	raħ	titsammaxo	kinto raħ	titsammaxo
Huwwi	xam	yitsammax	raħ	yitsammax	ken raħ	yitsammax
Hiyyi	xam	titsammax	raħ	titsammax	kenit raħ	titsammax
Hinni	xam	yitsammaxo	raħ	yitsammaxo	keno raħ	yitsammaxo
Niħna	xam	nitsammax	raħ	nitsammax	kinna raħ	nitsammax

Notes

This verb group is characterized by the double consonant before the last two letters. It is a very common verb group and memorizing it is advisable to any student of the Lebanese language.

Yitfarkac

Group: 9F

To tumble

Principal Forms

Pronoun	Infinitive	Simple Present	Perfect Present	Simple Past	Imperative
Ana	itfarkac	bitfarkac	mfarkac	tfarkact	
Inta	titfarkac	btitfarkac	mfarkac	tfarkact	tfarkac
Inti	titfarkaci	btitfarkaci	mfarkaci	tfarkacti	tfarkaci
Into	titfarkaco	btitfarkaco	mfarkaciin	tfarkacto	tfarkaco
Huwwi	yitfarkac	byitfarkac	mfarkac	tfarkac	
Hiyyi	titfarkac	btitfarkac	mfarkaci	tfarkacit	
Hinni	yitfarkaco	byitfarkaco	mfarkaciin	tfarkaco	
Niħna	nitfarkac	mnitfarkac	mfarkaciin	tfarkacna	

Past Tense Forms

Pronoun + To Be		Past Continuous		Past Habit	Past Perfect	Past Anterior
Ana	kint	xam	itfarkac	itfarkac	mfarkac	tfarkact
Inta	kint	xam	titfarkac	titfarkac	mfarkac	tfarkact
Inti	kinti	xam	titfarkaci	titfarkaci	mfarkaci	tfarkacti
Into	kinto	xam	titfarkaco	titfarkaco	mfarkaciin	tfarkacto
Huwwi	ken	xam	yitfarkac	yitfarkac	mfarkac	tfarkac
Hiyyi	kenit	xam	titfarkac	titfarkac	mfarkaci	tfarkacit
Hinni	keno	xam	yitfarkaco	yitfarkaco	mfarkaciin	tfarkaco
Niħna	kinna	xam	nitfarkac	nitfarkac	mfarkaciin	tfarkacna

Present and Future Tense Forms

Pronoun	Present Continuous		Simple Future		Anterior Future	
Ana	xam	itfarkac	raħ	itfarkac	kint raħ	itfarkac
Inta	xam	titfarkac	raħ	titfarkac	kint raħ	titfarkac
Inti	xam	titfarkaci	raħ	titfarkaci	kinti raħ	titfarkaci
Into	xam	titfarkaco	raħ	titfarkaco	kinto raħ	titfarkaco
Huwwi	xam	yitfarkac	raħ	yitfarkac	ken raħ	yitfarkac
Hiyyi	xam	titfarkac	raħ	titfarkac	kenit raħ	titfarkac
Hinni	xam	yitfarkaco	raħ	yitfarkaco	keno raħ	yitfarkaco
Niħna	xam	nitfarkac	raħ	nitfarkac	kinna raħ	nitfarkac

Notes

This verb group could be included under the previous verb group but is listed here separately for convenience to the student, since the infinitive does not have a double consonant.

Yitṡaarax

To wrestle

Group: 9G

Principal Forms

Pronoun	Infinitive	Simple Present	Perfect Present	Simple Past	Imperative
Ana	itṡaarax	bitṡaarax	mṡaarax	tṡaaraxt	
Inta	titṡaarax	btitṡaarax	mṡaarax	tṡaaraxt	tṡaarax
Inti	titṡaaraxi	btitṡaaraxi	mṡaaraxa	tṡaaraxti	tṡaaraxi
Into	titṡaaraxo	btitṡaaraxo	mṡaaraxiin	tṡaaraxto	tṡaaraxo
Huwwi	yitṡaarax	byitṡaarax	mṡaarax	tṡaarax	
Hiyyi	titṡaarax	btitṡaarax	mṡaaraxa	tṡaaraxit	
Hinni	yitṡaaraxo	byitṡaaraxo	mṡaaraxiin	tṡaaraxo	
Niħna	nitṡaarax	mnitṡaarax	mṡaaraxiin	tṡaaraxna	

Past Tense Forms

Pronoun + To Be		Past Continuous		Past Habit	Past Perfect	Past Anterior
Ana	kint	xam	itṡaarax	itṡaarax	mṡaarax	tṡaaraxt
Inta	kint	xam	titṡaarax	titṡaarax	mṡaarax	tṡaaraxt
Inti	kinti	xam	titṡaaraxi	titṡaaraxi	mṡaaraxa	tṡaaraxti
Into	kinto	xam	titṡaaraxo	titṡaaraxo	mṡaaraxiin	tṡaaraxto
Huwwi	ken	xam	yitṡaarax	yitṡaarax	mṡaarax	tṡaarax
Hiyyi	kenit	xam	titṡaarax	titṡaarax	mṡaaraxa	tṡaaraxit
Hinni	keno	xam	yitṡaaraxo	yitṡaaraxo	mṡaaraxiin	tṡaaraxo
Niħna	kinna	xam	nitṡaarax	nitṡaarax	mṡaaraxiin	tṡaaraxna

Present and Future Tense Forms

Pronoun	Present Continuous		Simple Future		Anterior Future	
Ana	xam	itṡaarax	raħ	itṡaarax	kint raħ	itṡaarax
Inta	xam	titṡaarax	raħ	titṡaarax	kint raħ	titṡaarax
Inti	xam	titṡaaraxi	raħ	titṡaaraxi	kinti raħ	titṡaaraxi
Into	xam	titṡaaraxo	raħ	titṡaaraxo	kinto raħ	titṡaaraxo
Huwwi	xam	yitṡaarax	raħ	yitṡaarax	ken raħ	yitṡaarax
Hiyyi	xam	titṡaarax	raħ	titṡaarax	kenit raħ	titṡaarax
Hinni	xam	yitṡaaraxo	raħ	yitṡaaraxo	keno raħ	yitṡaaraxo
Niħna	xam	nitṡaarax	raħ	nitṡaarax	kinna raħ	nitṡaarax

Notes
This is a very rare verb group. It is characterized by the “aa” vowel sound.

Verbs List

Below is a table of most commonly used verbs. The table presents these verbs in an alphabetical order based on the Lebanese Infinitive. The past tense is also shown, and each verb is indicated by group. When you locate the verb that you need, you can then go to the group page and replace the consonants in the example verb with the consonants for your verb in the group table. In this way, you will be able to conjugate any of these verbs in all their forms.

Infinitive Verb	Past Tense	Meaning	Group
y`aarin	aaran	to compare	7Fb
y`aaṡiṡ	aaṡaṡ	to punish	7Fb
y`aaṫix	aaṫax	to interrupt	7Fb
y`accir	accar	to peel	7Db
y`addi	adda	to perform, to suffice	6Db
y`addif	addaf	to paddle	7Db
y`addim	addam	to apply, to introduce, to present	7Db
y`addir	addar	to appreciate, to estimate	7Db
y`affi	affa	to skip	6Db
y`affil	affal	to lock	7Db
y`akkid	akkad	to confirm	7Db
y`aḱḱir	aḱḱar	to delay	7Db
y`allil	allal	to reduce	7Db
y`allix	allax	to launch	7Db
y`ammin	amman	to provide, to trust, to insure	7Db
y`arrir	arrar	to decide	7Db
y`aṡ`iṡ	aṡ`aṡ	to clip	7Eb
y`aṡṡim	aṡṡam	to divide	7Db
y`assir	assar	to affect, to influence	7Db
y`aṡṡir	aṡṡar	to shorten	7Db
y`aṫṫib	aṫṫab	to stitch	7Db
y`aṫṫix	aṫṫax	to skip	7Db
y`awwi	awwa	to strengthen	6Db
y`awwiṡ	awwaṡ	to shoot	7Db
y`ayyid	ayyad	to note, to support	7Db
y`ayyis	ayyas	to measure	7Db
y`emin	eman	to believe	6F
y`iḣḣ	aḣḣ	to cough	5Gb
y`iis	es	to measure	5Ha
y`inn	ann	to groan	5Gb

Infinitive Verb	Past Tense	Meaning	Group
y`orr	arr	to admit, to confess	5Ib
y`oṡṡ	aṡṡ	to cut	5Ib
y`ud	ed	to lead	4Ea
y`ul	el	to say	4Ea
y`um	em	to rise	4Ea
yaxmil	ximil	to do, to make	6A
yaxrif	xirif	to know	6A
yaxṫi	xaṫa	to give, to provide	5A
ybaccir	baccar	to preach	7Da
ybaħbic	baħbac	to dig	7Ea
ybahdil	bahdal	to offend, to insult	7Ea
ybaħli`	baħla`	to stare	7Ea
ybaḱcic	baḱcac	to tip	7Ea
yballic	ballac	to begin, start	7Da
yballiġ	ballaġ	to report	7Da
ybarġi	barġa	to screw	6E
ybarhin	barhan	to prove	7Ea
ybarmij	barmaj	to program	7Ea
ybarwiz	barwaz	to frame	7Ea
ybayyiḋ	bayyaḋ	to bleach	7Da
ybayyin	bayyan	to appear	7Da
yberik	berak	to bless	6F
ybiix	bex	to sell	5Ha
ybus	bes	to kiss	4Eb
yca``if	ca``af	to chop	7Da
ycaariṫ	caaraṫ	to bet	7Fa
ycabbiħ	cabbaħ	to boast	7Da
ycaħħim	caħħam	to grease	7Da
ycajjix	cajjax	to encourage	7Da
ycakkik	cakkak	to doubt	7Da
ycalliħ	callaħ	to strip	7Da
ycanḱir	canḱar	to snore	7Ea
ycatti	catta	to rain, to spend winter	6Da
ycaxcix	caxcax	to sparkle	7Ea
ycerik	cerak	to contribute, to share	6F
yci``	ca``	to crack	5Ga
ycidd	cadd	to pull, to stress	5Ga
yciil	cel	to remove	5Ha

Infinitive Verb	Past Tense	Meaning	Group
ycikk	cakk	to plug, to suspect	5Ga
ycimm	camm	to smell	5Ga
ycixx	caxx	to beam, to glow, to radiate	5Ga
ycuf	cef	to see	4Eb
ydabbir	dabbar	to manage	7Da
ydabdib	dabdab	to crawl	7Ea
ydaḱḱin	daḱḱan	to smoke	7Da
ydammir	dammar	to crush, to destroy	7Da
ydarrib	darrab	to coach, to train	7Da
ydawbil	dawbal	to double, to pass	7Ea
ydawwib	dawwab	to melt something, to thaw	7Da
ydawwir	dawwar	to turn on, to search	7Da
ydaxwis	daxwas	to stomp, to pedal	7Ea
ydayyin	dayyan	to lend money	7Da
ydefix	defax	to defend	6F
ydekic	dekac	to barter, to trade	6F
ydewi	dewa	to medicate, to mend	5K
ydeyi`	deya`	to annoy, to harass	6F
ydi``	da``	to hammer, to knock, to tap	5Ga
ydii`	de`	to become tight	5Ha
ydiin	den	to condemn	5Ha
ydill	dall	to point, to indicate	5Ga
ydu`	de`	to taste	4Ea
ydub	deb	to melt	4Eb
yduḱ	deḱ	to become dizzy	4Eb
yḋaayin	ḋaayan	to last	7Fa
yḋall	ḋall	to remain	5Gc
yḋawwi	ḋawwa	to turn the light on	6E
yḋayyix	ḋayyax	to lose, to waste	7Da
yḋobb	ḋabb	to pack	5Ia
yḋoḱḱ	ḋaḱḱ	to pump	5Ia
yḋomm	ḋamm	to include	5Ia
yeḱod	aḱad	to take	5B
yekol	akal	to eat	5B
yfackil	fackal	to mess up	7Ea
yfaḋḋi	faḋḋa	to empty	6Da
yfaḋḋil	faḋḋal	prefer	7Da
yfajjir	fajjar	to bomb	7Da

Infinitive Verb	Past Tense	Meaning	Group
yfakfik	fakfak	to dismantle	7Ea
yfakkir	fakkar	to think	7Da
yfallit	fallat	to release	7Da
yfar`ix	far`ax	to pop	7Ea
yfarci	farca	to brush	6E
yfarfiṫ	farfaṫ	to scatter	7Ea
yfarji	farja	to show	6E
yfarriḱ	farraḱ	to sprout	7Da
yfassir	fassar	to explain	7Da
yfattic	fattac	to search	7Da
yfawwiḣ	fawwaḣ	to rinse	7Da
yfayyi	fayya	to shade	6Da
yfazzix	fazzax	to scare	7Da
yfeji`	feja`	to surprise	6F
yfiiḋ	faaḋ	to overflow	5Hb
yfikk	fakk	to untie, to unfasten, to unscrew	5Ga
yfill	fall	to leave	5Ga
yfitt	fatt	to deal	5Ga
yfizz	fazz	to hop, to jump	5Ga
yfuc	fec	to float	4Eb
yfut	fet	to enter	4Eb
yġanni	ġanna	to sing	6Da
yġarri`	ġarra`	to drown	7Da
yġassil	ġassal	to wash	7Da
yġaṫṫi	ġaṫṫa	to cover	6Da
yġayyir	ġayyar	to change	7Da
yġicc	ġacc	to cheat	5Ga
yġoṡṡ	ġaṡṡ	to choke	5Ia
yġoṫṫ	ġaṫṫ	to land	5Ia
yhaddi	hadda	to hold	6Da
yhaddid	haddad	to threaten	7Da
yhallil	hallal	to rejoice	7Da
yhanni	hanna	to congratulate	6Da
yharwil	harwal	to jog	7Ea
yhayyij	hayyaj	to excite	7Da
yhejim	hejam	to attack	6F
yhimm	hamm	to matter, to trouble, to concern	5Ga
yhizz	hazz	to shake, to nod	5Ga

Infinitive Verb	Past Tense	Meaning	Group
yħa``i`	ħa``a`	to achieve	7Da
yħaawiṫ	ħaawaṫ	to surround	7Fa
yħaddid	ħaddad	to locate, to mark, to spot	7Da
yħaḋḋir	ħaḋḋar	to prepare	7Da
yħallil	ħallal	to analyze	7Da
yħammi	ħamma	to warm	6Da
yħammil	ħammal	to load	7Da
yħammis	ħammas	to cheer	7Da
yħarrik	ħarrak	to stir	7Da
yħarrim	ħarram	to ban	7Da
yħarrir	ħarrar	to free	7Da
yħaṡṡin	ħassan	to improve	7Da
yħerib	ħerab	to fight (in a war), to battle	6F
yħewil	ħewal	to try, to attempt	6F
yħibb	ħabb	to like, to love	5Ga
yħidd	ħadd	to limit, to mourn	5Ga
yħiff	ħaff	to rub, to scrub	5Ga
yħikk	ħakk	to scratch	5Ga
yħiss	ħass	to feel	5Ga
yħoṫṫ	ħaṫṫ	to place, to put	5Ia
yi`bal	ibil	to accept	6Gb
yi`cax	icix	to see	6Gb
yi`daħ	adaħ	to spark, to drill	6Bb
yi`dar	idir	to afford, to be able	6Gb
yi`la`	ili`	to worry	6Gb
yi`li	ala	to fry	5Db
yi`lob	alab	to switch, to tumble	6Jb
yi`ra	iri	to read	5Eb
yi`sa	isi	to harden	5Eb
yi`ṫiriħ	`ṫaraħ	to suggest	8Aa
yi`tol	atal	to kill, to murder	6Jb
yi`wi	awa	to shelter	5Db
yi`xod	axad	to settle, to sit	6Jb
yi`zi	aza	to harm	5Db
yib`a	bi`i	to stay	5Ea
yibda	bidi	to start	5Ea
yibdol	badal	to replace	6Ja
yibki	biki	to cry	5C

Infinitive Verb	Past Tense	Meaning	Group
yibḱac	baḱac	to puncture	6Ba
yibroz	baraz	to reveal	6Ja
yibtisim	btasam	to smile	8Aa
yibxat	baxat	to send	6Ba
yicbok	cabak	to pin, to cross	6Ja
yicfi	cafa	to heal	5Da
yicħad	caħad	to beg	6Ba
yickor	cakar	to thank	6Ja
yiclaħ	calaħ	to undress	6Ba
yicmol	camal	to include	6Ja
yicrab	cirib	to drink	6Ga
yicte`	cte`	to long for, to miss	6I
yictiġil	ctaġal	to work	8Aa
yictili`	ctala`	to realize	8Aa
yictiri	ctara	to buy	7A
yiddixi	ddaxa	to claim	7A
yidfax	dafax	to pay	6Ba
yidfoc	dafac	to push	6Ja
yidhan	dahan	to paint	6Ba
yidros	daras	to study	6Ja
yidxas	daxas	to step	6Ba
yifcal	ficil	to fail	6Ga
yifham	fihim	to understand	6Ga
yiftaħ	fataħ	to open, to unlock	6Ba
yiftikir	ftakar	to regard, to suppose	8Aa
yiftiri`	ftara`	to part	8Aa
yiftol	fatal	to twist	6Ja
yiġli	ġili	to boil	5C
yiġlo`	ġala`	to close the door	6Ja
yiġmoz	ġamaz	to wink	6Ja
yiġra`	ġiri`	to drown	6Ga
yiġtel	ġtel	to assassinate	6I
yiġwi	ġiwi	to tempt	5C
yihjom	hajam	to attack	6Ja
yihtamm	htamm	to care, to be concerned, to take interest	7B
yiħ`on	ħa`an	to inject	6Ja
yiħbos	ħabas	to jail	6Ja
yiħci	ħaca	to stuff	5Da

Infinitive Verb	Past Tense	Meaning	Group
yiħjoz	ħajaz	to book	6Ja
yiħki	ħiki	to speak, to talk	5C
yiħkom	ħakam	to judge, to reign, to rule	6Ja
yiħlam	ħilim	to dream	6Ga
yiħlo`	ħala`	to shave	6Ja
yiħlob	ħalab	to milk	6Ja
yiħlof	ħalaf	to swear	6Ja
yiħmol	ħimil	to carry	6Jc
yiħro`	ħara`	to burn	6Ja
yiħrok	ħarak	to move	6Ja
yiħros	ħaras	to guard	6Ja
yiħsob	ħasab	to calculate	6Ja
yiħtajj	ħtajj	to complain	7B
yiħzar	ħizir	to guess	6Bb
yii`as	yi`is	to become depressed	6H
yiji	ija	to come	4A
yijlod	jalad	to whip	6Ja
yijmax	jamax	to gather, to add	6Ba
yijni	jini	to earn	5C
yijrod	jarad	to scrape	6Ja
yijwi	jawa	to dirty, to stain	5Da
yijxar	jaxar	to scream, to shout loudly	6Ba
yijzob	jazab	to attract	6Ja
yikbar	kibir	to grow	6Ga
yikbos	kabas	to press, to pickle	6Ja
yikmoc	kamac	to catch	6Ja
yikrah	kirih	to hate	6Ga
yiksor	kasar	to break	6Ja
yikticif	ktacaf	to discover	8Aa
yiktob	katab	to write	6Ja
yiḱboz	ḱabaz	to bake	6Ja
yiḱdax	ḱadax	to fool, to trick	6Ba
yiḱdom	ḱadam	to serve	6Ja
yiḱjal	ḱijil	to blush	6Ga
yiḱla`	ḱala`	to create	6Ba
yiḱsar	ḱisir	to lose	6Ga
yiḱtibir	ḱtabar	to experience	8Aa
yiḱtifi	ḱtafa	to disappear, to fade, to vanish	7A

Infinitive Verb	Past Tense	Meaning	Group
yiḱtilif	ḱtalaf	to disagree	8Aa
yiḱtirix	ḱtarax	to invent	8Aa
yiḱtom	ḱatam	to seal, to stamp	6Ja
yiḱzo`	ḱaza`	to tear	6Ja
yilbos	libis	to wear	6Jc
yilġi	laġa	to cancel	5Da
yilħa`	liħi`	to chase, to follow	6Ga
yilħas	laħas	to lick	6Ba
yiltazz	ltazz	to savor	7B
yiltizim	ltazam	to commit	8Aa
yilwi	lawa	to bend	5Da
yilxab	lixib	to play	6Ga
yilzom	lazam	to obligate	6Ja
yimci	mici	to walk, to march	5C
yimlok	malak	to own, to posses	6Ja
yimnax	manax	to prevent	6Ba
yimsaħ	masaħ	to wipe	6Ba
yimsok	misik	to grab, to hold	6Jc
yimtiħin	mtaħan	to test	8Aa
yimtilik	mtalak	to have	8Aa
yimxas	maxas	to squash	6Ba
yimzaħ	mazaħ	to joke	6Ba
yin`ax	na`ax	to soak	6Ba
yin`ol	na`al	to transport, to transfer	6Ja
yindam	nidim	to regret	6Ga
yinfi	nafa	to deny	5Da
yinfijir	nfajar	to explode	8Aa
yinfilic	nfalac	to spread	8Aa
yinfoḱ	nafaḱ	to blow	6Ja
yinfor	nafar	to dislike	6Ja
yinhi	naha	to end	5Da
yinħat	naħat	to carve	6Ba
yinħini	nħana	to bow	7A
yinja	niji	to survive	5Ea
yinjaħ	najaħ	to succeed	6Ba
yinjeb	njeb	to be brought	6I
yinkisir	nkasar	to be broken	8Aa
yinkoz	nakaz	to poke	6Ja

Infinitive Verb	Past Tense	Meaning	Group
yinsa	nisi	to forget	5Ea
yinsaḱ	nasaḱ	to copy	6Ba
yintibih	ntabah	to notice	8Aa
yintiḱib	ntaḱab	to vote	8Aa
yintimi	ntama	to belong	7A
yintoj	nataj	to produce	6Ja
yinwijid	nwajad	to exist	8Aa
yinxijib	nxajab	to fancy	8Aa
yinzal	nizil	to descend	6Ga
yinzax	nazax	to damage, to ruin, to spoil	6Ba
yirbaħ	ribiħ	to gain, to win	6Ga
yirġi	riġi	to foam	5C
yirjax	rijix	to return	6Ga
yirjof	rajaf	to shiver, to tremble	6Ja
yirkab	rikib	to ride	6Ga
yirkax	rakax	to kneel	6Ba
yirkod	rakad	to stagnate	6Ja
yirkoḋ	rakaḋ	to run	6Ja
yirmi	rama	to throw	5Da
yirsi	risi	to moor	5C
yirsom	rasam	to draw	6Ja
yirteħ	rteħ	to relax, to rest	6I
yirtifix	rtafax	to ascend	8Aa
yirxa	rixi	to itch	5Ea
yis`al	sa`al	to ask	6Ba
yisbaħ	sabaħ	to swim	6Ba
yisfo`	safa`	to slap	6Ja
yisħab	saħab	to pull	6Ba
yiskon	sakan	to dwell	6Ja
yiskot	sakat	to be silent	6Ja
yismaħ	samaħ	to allow, to permit	6Ba
yismax	simix	to hear	6Bb
yisnod	sanad	to support	6Ja
yisro`	sara`	to steal, to rob	6Ja
yista`bil	sta`bal	to receive, to welcome	9A
yista`jir	sta`jar	to rent	9A
yista`zin	sta`zan	to excuse oneself	9A
yistabidd	stabadd	to domineer	9C

Infinitive Verb	Past Tense	Meaning	Group
yistafiid	stafed	to profit	9B
yistaħli	staħla	to desire	8B
yistajimm	stajamm	to relax	9C
yistarji	starja	to dare	8B
yistawxib	stawxab	to contain	9A
yistaxdi	staxda	to become an enemy of	8B
yistaxidd	staxadd	to get ready	9C
yistaxiir	staxer	to borrow	9B
yistaxjil	staxjal	to rush	9A
yistaxmil	staxmal	to use	9A
yistehil	stehal	to deserve	8Db
yistilim	stalam	to receive	8Aa
yistwa``a	stwa``a	to be careful	9D
yistxiir	stxer	to borrow	8E
yiṡ`i	ṡa`a	to water	5Da
yit`addam	t`addam	to precede	9E
yit`assaf	t`assaf	to regret	9E
yit`exad	t`exad	to retire	8Da
yitbeḱal	tbeḱal	to be skimpy	8Da
yitbelad	tbelad	to act lazy	8Da
yitca`lab	tca`lab	to roll, to tumble	9F
yitcakka	tcakka	to complain	8C
yitdaffa`	tdaffa`	to flow	9E
yitḋaħħak	tḋaħħak	to laugh	9E
yitdaḱḱal	tdaḱḱal	to interfere	9E
yitdarkab	tdarkab	to tumble	9E
yitfa``ad	tfa``ad	to check	9E
yitfarkac	tfarkac	to trip	9F
yitfarraj	tfarraj	to watch	9E
yitfarrax	tfarrax	to branch	9E
yitfeda	tfeda	to dodge, to avoid	7C
yitġadda	tġadda	to have lunch	8C
yitħaccar	tħaccar	to meddle	9E
yitħadda	tħadda	to challenge	8C
yithajja	thajja	to spell	8C
yitħakkam	tħakkam	to control	9E
yitħammam	tħammam	to bathe	9E
yitħarra	tħarra	to detect	8C

Infinitive Verb	Past Tense	Meaning	Group
yitħarrak	tħarrak	to move	9E
yitjalla	tjalla	to materialize	8C
yitjannab	tjannab	to avoid	9E
yitjawwaz	tjawwaz	to marry	9E
yitjedal	tjedal	to argue	8Da
yitjehal	tjehal	to ignore	8Da
yitḱabba	tḱabba	to hide	8C
yitkawwan	tkawwan	consist, to come into being, to take form	9E
yitḱena`	tḱena`	to fight	8Da
yitketar	tketar	to reproduce, to multiply	8Da
yitḱeyal	tḱeyal	to imagine	8Da
yitle`a	tle`a	to meet	7C
yitloj	talaj	to snow	6Ja
yitmanna	tmanna	to hope, to wish	8C
yitmarran	tmarran	to exercise, to practice	9E
yitna`waz	tna`waz	to peep	9F
yitnaffas	tnaffas	to breathe	9E
yitnahhad	tnahhad	to sigh	9E
yitnefas	tnefas	to compete	8Da
yitrawwa`	trawwa`	to have breakfast	9E
yitṡaarax	tṡaarax	to wrestle	9G
yitsammax	tsammax	to listen	9E
yitṡarraf	tṡarraf	to behave	9E
yitṡaṫṫaħ	tṡaṫṫaħ	to lay	9E
yitsawwa`	tsawwa`	to shop	9E
yitṡayyad	tṡayyad	to hunt	9E
yitse`al	tse`al	to question, to wonder	8Da
yitṫallab	tṫallab	to require	9E
yitṫallax	tṫallax	to look	9E
yitṫawwar	tṫawwar	to develop, to evolve	9E
yittewab	ttewab	to yawn	8Da
yittikil	ttakal	to rely	8Aa
yitṫoṡil	tṫaṡal	to contact	8Ab
yitwa``a	twa``a	to be careful	8C
yitwa``ax	twa``ax	to expect	9E
yitwajjah	twajjah	to head	9E
yitwassax	twassax	to expand	9E
yitṫwi	ṫawa	to fold	5Da

Infinitive Verb	Past Tense	Meaning	Group
yitxacca	txacca	to have dinner	8C
yitxajjab	txajjab	to wonder	9E
yitxalla`	txalla`	to get attached to, to hang unto	9E
yitxallam	txallam	to learn	9E
yitxarraf	txarraf	to recognize, to identify	9E
yitxazzab	txazzab	to suffer	9E
yitzakkar	tzakkar	to remember	9E
yitzallaj	tzallaj	to ski	9E
yitzammar	tzammar	to complain	9E
yitzeka	tzeka	to act intelligent (in a negative way)	7C
yitzewaj	tzewaj	to mate	8Da
yitżaahar	tżaahar	to pretend	9E
yix`od	xa`ad	to knot	6Ja
yixfi	xifi	to spare, to pardon	5C
yixjob	xajab	to be admired, to impress	6Ja
yixkos	xakas	to reflect	6Ja
yixlok	xalak	to chew	6Ja
yixlon	axlan	to announce, to broadcast	6Ja
yixmi	xama	to blind	5Da
yixni	xini	to mean	5C
yixtibir	xtabar	to consider	8Aa
yixtimid	xtamad	to depend	8Aa
yixtini	xtana	to tend to, to care for	7A
yixtirif	xtaraf	to confess	8Aa
yixtizir	xtazar	to apologize	8Aa
yixṫoriḋ	xṫaraḋ	to object	8Ab
yixzom	xazam	to invite someone	6Ja
yizkor	zakar	to mention	6Ja
yizxoj	zaxaj	to annoy, to irritate someone	6Ja
yjallid	jallad	to freeze something	7Da
yjammix	jammax	to collect, to gather	7Da
yjarrib	jarrab	to try	7Da
yjarrid	jarrad	to disarm	7Da
yjaxxid	jaxxad	to curl	7Da
yjedil	jedal	to argue	6F
yjewib	jewab	to answer	6F
yjiib	jeb	to bring, to get, to fetch	5Ha
yjirr	jarr	to drag	5Ga

Infinitive Verb	Past Tense	Meaning	Group
ykabbir	kabbar	to enlarge, to make bigger	7Da
ykaccir	kaccar	to frown	7Da
ykaddis	kaddas	to pile	7Da
ykallif	kallaf	to cost, to assign	7Da
ykammil	kammal	to continue	7Da
ykassir	kassar	to wreck	7Da
ykawwix	kawwax	to curve	7Da
ykazdir	kazdar	to tour, to wander	7Ea
ykazzib	kazzab	to lie	7Da
ykizz	kazz	to trace a drawing or copy a text	5Ga
ykun	ken	to be	4Eb
yḱabbir	ḱabbar	to inform, to tell	7Da
yḱaffif	ḱaffaf	to lighten, to slow	7Da
yḱajjil	ḱajjal	to embarrass	7Da
yḱalli	ḱalla	to allow, to keep, to let	6Da
yḱallif	ḱallaf	to give birth to	7Da
yḱalliṡ	ḱallaṡ	to complete, to finish, to rescue, to save	7Da
yḱarbic	ḱarbac	to scribble	7Ea
yḱarrib	ḱarrab	to damage	7Da
yḱaṫṫiṫ	ḱaṫṫaṫ	to plan	7Da
yḱawwif	ḱawwaf	to frighten, terrify	7Da
yḱayyim	ḱayyam	to camp	7Da
yḱayyiṫ	ḱayyaṫ	to saw, to knit	7Da
yḱazzin	ḱazzan	to store	7Da
yḱef	ḱef	to fear	4D
yḱelif	ḱelaf	to disapprove, to infringe	6F
ylabbis	labbas	to dress someone	7Da
ylaḱbiṫ	laḱbaṫ	to confuse	7Ea
ylammix	lammax	to polish	7Da
ylawwin	lawwan	to color	7Da
ylazzi`	lazza`	to tape, to paste, to attach, to glue	7Da
yle`i	le`a	to find	5K
yliff	laff	to coil, to wrap	5Ga
ymacciṫ	maccaṫ	to comb	7Da
ymakkin	makkan	to enable someone	7Da
ymarḣib	marḣab	to greet, to wave, to welcome	7Ea
ymarrin	marran	to train	7Da
ymasmir	masmar	to nail	7Ea

Infinitive Verb	Past Tense	Meaning	Group
ymassiħ	massaħ	to wipe, to swipe, to dust	7Da
ymassil	massal	to act, to represent	7Da
ymazmiz	mazmaz	to sip	7Ea
ymenix	menax	to mind	6F
ymoṡṡ	maṡṡ	to suck	5Ia
ymut	met	to die	4Eb
yna``i	na``a	to choose, to pick	6Da
yna``ib	na``ab	to mine	7Da
yna``iṡ	na``aṡ	to reduce, to subtract	7Da
yna``iṫ	na``aṫ	to drip	7Da
ynaa`iṡ	naa`aṡ	to bid	7Fa
ynabbih	nabbah	to alert, to warn	7Da
ynaccif	naccaf	to dry	7Da
ynaḋḋif	naḋḋaf	to clean	7Da
ynaṫniṫ	naṫnaṫ	to bounce	7Ea
ynaycin	naycan	to aim with a gun	7Ea
ynażżim	nażżam	to organize	7Da
yne`ic	ne`ac	to discuss	6F
ynedi	neda	to call	5K
ynem	nem	to sleep	4D
ynesib	nesab	to suit	6F
yni``	na``	to nag, to whine	5Ga
yo`baḋ	abaḋ	to collect money	6Bd
yo`har	ahar	to tease	6Bd
yo`mor	amar	to order, to command	6Cb
yo`roṡ	araṡ	to pinch	6Cb
yo`ṡod	aṡad	to intend	6Cb
yo`ṡom	aṡam	to split	6Cb
yo`ṫax	aṫax	to pass	6Bd
yo`ṫor	aṫar	to tow	6Cb
yobħar	baħar	to sail	6Bc
yobrom	baram	to turn	6Ca
yobṡoṫ	baṡaṫ	to please	6Ca
yod`ar	da`ar	to touch	6Bc
yoḋboṫ	ḋabaṫ	to set	6Ca
yoḋman	ḋaman	to guarantee	6Bc
yoḋrob	ḋarab	to hit, to beat, to multiply (math)	6Ca
yofħaṡ	faħaṡ	to examine	6Bc

Infinitive Verb	Past Tense	Meaning	Group
yofṡol	faṡal	to separate	6Ca
yoġdor	ġadar	to foul, to deceive	6Ca
yoġlaṫ	ġoliṫ	to make a mistake	6Be
yoġtoṡ	ġaṫaṡ	to dive	6Ca
yoħḋar	ħoḋir	to watch television, to attend	6Be
yoħfaż	ħafaż	to preserve, to memorize	6Bc
yoħfor	ħafar	to dig	6Bc
yohjor	hajar	to abandon, to desert	6Ca
yohrob	harab	to escape	6Ca
yoħṡal	ħaṡal	to obtain	6Bc
yoj`or	ja`ar	to gaze	6Ca
yojbor	jabar	to force	6Ca
yojraħ	jaraħ	to injure	6Bc
yoḱlaṡ	ḱalaṡ	to finish	6Bc
yoḱloṫ	ḱalaṫ	to mix	6Ca
yoḱṫor	ḱaṫar	to come to mind	6Ca
yoḱṫi	ḱoṫi	to sin	5Fa
yoḱṫof	ḱaṫaf	to kidnap	6Ca
yol`aṫ	la`aṫ	to catch, to arrest	6Bc
yolboṫ	labaṫ	to kick	6Ca
yomḋi	moḋi	to sign	5Fb
yomġaṫ	maġaṫ	to stretch	6Bc
yon`or	na`ar	to drill through	6Ca
yonboṡiṫ	nbaṡaṫ	to enjoy, to be happy	8Ab
yoncor	nacar	to post, to publish, to saw	6Ca
yonṡaħ	naṡaħ	to advise	6Bc
yonṫor	naṫar	to wait	6Ca
yor`oṡ	ra`aṡ	to dance	6Ca
yorboṫ	rabaṫ	to knot, to tie, to connect	6Ca
yorḋi	riḋi	to satisfy	5Fb
yorfax	rafax	to raise	6Bc
yorfoḋ	rafaḋ	to refuse, to reject	6Ca
yoṡ`i	ṡa`a	to water	5Fa
yoṡ`oṫ	ṡa`aṫ	to fail, to fall	6Ca
yoṡḋom	ṡaḋam	to shock	6Ca
yoṡrof	ṡaraf	to spend	6Ca
yoṡroḱ	ṡaraḱ	to scream	6Ca
yoṫbax	ṫabax	to print, to type	6Bc

Infinitive Verb	Past Tense	Meaning	Group
yoṫboḱ	ṫabaḱ	to cook	6Ca
yoṫfi	ṫafa	to turn off	5Fa
yoṫlob	ṫalab	to request	6Ca
yoṫroḋ	ṫaraḋ	to expel, to fire, to kick out	6Ca
yoxboṫ	xabaṫ	to hug	6Ca
yoxroḋ	xaraḋ	to offer	6Ca
yoxṡor	xaṡar	to juice, to squeeze	6Ca
yoxṫob	xaṫab	to damage, to bruise	6Ca
yoxṫoṡ	xaṫas	to sneeze	6Ca
yożħaṫ	żaħaṫ	to slip	6Bc
yożrax	żarax	to plant	6Bc
yra``im	ra``am	to number	7Da
yraḱḱiṡ	raḱḱaṡ	to reduce the price, to license	7Da
yrakkiz	rakkaz	to concentrate, to set in a foundation	7Da
yrattib	rattab	to organize, to arrange	7Da
yrawwi`	rawwa`	to calm someone, to soothe someone	7Da
yrawwiḋ	rawwaḋ	to tame	7Da
yre`ib	re`ab	to observe	6F
yricc	racc	to spray	5Ga
yridd	radd	to reply, to return	5Ga
yrinn	rann	to ring	5Ga
yroff	raff	to blink	5Ia
yruħ	raaħ	to go	4F
ysabbib	sabbab	to cause	7Da
ysaddi`	sadda`	to believe	7Da
ysajjil	sajjal	to record	7Da
ysakkir	sakkar	to close	7Da
ysalli	salla	to amuse, to entertain	6Da
ysallim	sallam	to greet, to hand something to someone	7Da
ysammi	samma	to name	6Da
ysebi`	seba`	to race	6F
ysefir	sefar	to travel	6F
ysemiħ	semaħ	to forgive	6F
ysenid	senad	to support, to back someone up	6F
ysewi	sewa	to fix	5K
ysex	sex	to fit	4D
ysexid	sexad	to help	6F
yseyif	seyaf	to fence with a sword	6F

Infinitive Verb	Past Tense	Meaning	Group
ysidd	sadd	to seal, to plug, to close, to dam	5Ga
ysu`	se`	to drive, to steer	4Eb
yṡaḱḱin	ṡaḱḱan	to heat, to warm up	7Da
yṡalli	ṡalla	to pray	6Da
yṡalliḣ	ṡallaḣ	to correct	7Da
yṡammim	ṡammam	to design	7Da
yṡannif	ṡannaf	to categorize	7Da
yṡarrif	ṡarraf	to conjugate, to exchange money	7Da
yṡarriḱ	ṡarraḱ	to shout, to scream	7Da
yṡawfir	ṡawfar	to whistle	7Ea
yṡawṡi	ṡawṡa	to squeak	6E
yṡawwir	ṡawwar	to take a photo, to film a movie	7Da
yṡiir	ṡaar	to become, to happen, to occur	5Hb
yṡobb	ṡabb	to pour	5Ia
yṡoff	ṡaff	to park	5Ia
yṡoḣḣ	ṡaḣḣ	to cure	5Ia
ytalfin	talfan	to call	7Ea
ytarjim	tarjam	to translate	7Ea
ytaxxib	taxxab	to make someone tired	7Da
yṫabbic	ṫabbac	to pat someone's back	7Da
yṫabbil	ṫabbal	to drum	7Da
yṫaḣbic	ṫaḣbac	to crash, to smash	7Ea
yṫawwil	ṫawwal	to lengthen	7Da
yṫaxmi	ṫaxma	to feed	6E
yṫiir	ṫaar	to fly	5Hb
yṫiix	ṫaax	to obey	5Hb
ytikk	takk	to tick	5Ga
yṫomm	ṫamm	to fill a hole with dirt	5Ia
yṫuf	ṫaaf	to flood, to hover, to travel around	4F
yu`af	wi`if	to stand	5Ja
yu`ax	wi`ix	to fall	5Ja
yufi	wafa	to honor a promise	4Ba
yujax	wijix	to feel pain	5Ja
yumi	wimi	to insinuate, to signal	4Bb
yuṡal	wuṡil	to arrive	5Ja
yuṡof	waṡaf	to describe	5Jb
yuṡol	waṡal	to join, to link	5Jb
yuxa	wixi	to wake up	4C

Infinitive Verb	Past Tense	Meaning	Group
yuxod	waxad	to promise	5Jb
yuzor	wazar	to jam	5Jb
ywa``if	wa``af	to stop, to suspend	7Da
ywa``ix	wa``ax	to drop	7Da
ywabbiḱ	wabbaḱ	to scold	7Da
ywacwic	wacwac	to whisper	7Ea
ywaḋḋiḣ	waḋḋaḣ	to clarify	7Da
ywaffi`	waffa`	to reconcile, to match	7Da
ywaffir	waffar	to save, to supply	7Da
ywaḣḣid	waḣḣad	to unite	7Da
ywajjih	wajjah	to guide	7Da
ywajjix	wajjax	to hurt	7Da
ywallix	wallax	to burn	7Da
ywalwil	walwal	to wail	7Ea
ywassiḱ	wassaḱ	to soil, to make something dirty	7Da
ywassix	wassax	to extend	7Da
ywaṡṡil	waṡṡal	to deliver, to reach	7Da
ywaxxi	waxxa	to wake someone up	6Da
yważżif	ważżaf	to employ	7Da
ywefi`	wefa`	to agree, to approve	6F
ywejih	wejah	to face	6F
ywezin	wezan	to balance	6F
yxabbi	xabba	to fill	6Da
yxabbir	xabbar	to express	7Da
yxacxic	xacxac	to nest	7Ea
yxaḋḋ	xaḋḋ	to bite	5Gc
yxaddid	xaddad	to list	7Da
yxaffin	xaffan	to mold, to decay, to rot	7Da
yxajjil	xajjal	to hurry	7Da
yxalli	xalla	to raise, to elevate	6Da
yxalli`	xalla`	to hang, to hook	7Da
yxallib	xallab	to box	7Da
yxallim	xallam	to educate, to mark, to teach	7Da
yxammir	xammar	to build	7Da
yxanwin	xanwan	to label	7Ea
yxarbic	xarbac	to climb	7Ea
yxarrif	xarraf	to make someone confess (church)	7Da
yxawkir	xawkar	to muddle	7Ea

Infinitive Verb	Past Tense	Meaning	Group
yxawwi	xawwa	to bark	6Da
yxawwi`	xawwa`	to be late, to delay	7Da
yxayyiṫ	xayyaṫ	to yell	7Da
yxelij	xelaj	to handle	6F
yxemil	xemal	to treat	6F
yxidd	xadd	to count	5Ga
yxiic	xec	to live	5Ha
yxiid	xed	to repeat, to redo	5Ha
yxiir	xer	to lend	5Ha
yxinn	xann	to hum, to moan	5Ga
yxuz	xez	to need, to want	4Eb
yya``is	ya``as	to depress someone else	7Da
yza``if	za``af	to clap, to applaud	7Da
yżabbiṫ	żabbaṫ	to repair	7Da
yżaġġir	żaġġar	to shrink, to make small	7Da
yzahhi`	zahha`	to bore	7Da
yzahhir	zahhar	to flower	7Da
yzakkir	zakkar	to remind	7Da
yzakzik	zakzak	to tickle	7Ea
yzaybi`	zayba`	to level	7Ea
yzayyin	zayyan	to decorate	7Da
yziid	zed	to add, to increase	5Ha
yziin	zen	to weigh	5Ha
yzijj	zajj	to involve	5Ga
yzur	zaar	to visit	4F

17259180R00060

Made in the USA
Charleston, SC
03 February 2013